Advance Praise for

"Explosive, penetrating, and utterly compelling, Kuhner charts the death spiral of American democracy as it collapses into the black hole of the religion of money. Never before in human history have noble ideals been corrupted so deeply with the connivance of so many. This book lays tyranny bare for all to see—as a mirror for the human soul."

 —Philip Goodchild, author of
  Theology of Money and *Credit and Faith*

"Timothy Kuhner captures the essence of Donald Trump—and modern American politics—in this illuminating book. Trump is many things but above all he is the embodiment of greed. To fix American democracy, Trump's defeat won't be enough. Instead, we'll have to rebuild the wall between private capital and public power."

 —Nicholas Stephanopoulos, Harvard Law School

"A learned and exceptionally creative meditation on our current predicament and our current president. Kuhner looks at Donald Trump, and the system that produced him, through the lenses of history, literature, philosophy, and theology. The result is explosive and vitally important."

 —H. N. Hirsch, Oberlin College

"In the span of a few years we have gone from arguing over politics, to arguing about how many tens of thousands of deaths would be worth boosting the stock market. We have become accustomed to wearing surgical masks to protect us from pandemics, and gas masks to protect us from riot police. If you're as worried about the effects of Trump's election as I am, then this brave and surprising book is for you. Kuhner locates not only the underlying causes of the crisis, but also the strength we need to overcome it."
—Reza Aslan, author of *Zealot: The Life and Times of Jesus of Nazareth*

"Timothy Kuhner masterfully situates Trump's presidency in broad historical perspective. He explains how and why so many Americans have come to tolerate and justify a plutocratic system with the values of greed and corruption that it sanctions. Kuhner's penetrating analysis calculates the enormous costs of our ideological complacency in spiritual, psychological, legal, cultural, and environmental terms. Everyone should heed his call for a revolutionary solution."
—John T. Jost, author of *A Theory of System Justification*

"A fabulous read! If you want to know why Trump is a demon and, more importantly, why that demon also lies within us and our politics, you must read this book."
—Joo-Cheong Tham, Melbourne Law School

TYRANNY OF GREED

TYRANNY OF GREED

Trump, Corruption, and the Revolution to Come

TIMOTHY K. KUHNER

stanford briefs
An Imprint of Stanford University Press
Stanford, California

Stanford University Press
Stanford, California

Printed in the United States of America
on acid-free, archival-quality paper

Library of Congress Cataloging-in-Publication Data

Names: Kuhner, Timothy K., author.
Title: Tyranny of greed : Trump, corruption, and the revolution to
    come / Timothy K. Kuhner.
Description: Stanford, California : Stanford Briefs an imprint of
    Stanford University Press, 2020. | Includes bibliographical
    references.
Identifiers: LCCN 2020019960 (print) | LCCN 2020019961 (ebook) |
    ISBN 9781503608504 (paperback) | ISBN 9781503614024 (epub)
Subjects: LCSH: Trump, Donald, 1946– | Political corruption—
    United States. | Plutocracy—United States. | Avarice—Political
    aspects—United States. | Democracy—United States. | United
    States—Politics and government—2017–
Classification: LCC E912 .K84 2020 (print) | LCC E912 (ebook) |
    DDC 973.933—dc23
LC record available at https://lccn.loc.gov/2020019960
LC ebook record available at https://lccn.loc.gov/2020019961

Cover design: Amanda Weiss

Typeset by Classic Typography in 11/15 Adobe Garamond

CONTENTS

PREFACE

Thus far, the twenty-first century is thrashing humanity with a sort of violence generally confined to science fiction or biblical times.

Even before the COVID-19 pandemic, a global catastrophe was well underway. Political analysts warned of democratic decline and rising authoritarianism. Economists uncovered alarming levels of inequality and capital concentration. Sociologists noted a resurgence in racism, sexism, and xenophobia. Scientists documented extreme temperature fluctuations, natural disasters, and an ongoing mass extinction. But in contrast to the pandemic, there has been no serious response to our social and environmental disintegration.

How could there be? The force that's ravaging the world is bound up with our way of life—with our values and belief systems, our economies and technologies, the laws we've passed (and failed to pass), and the leaders we've elected. So long as those leaders claim to understand our problems and to be doing something about them, most of us keep going about our lives without any serious change in worldview or behavior. We banish our lucid thoughts from the stage to the balcony. There, looking down on the characters in some futuristic dystopia or time-worn tragedy, our conscious awareness disassociates itself from humanity's plight.

This coping mechanism has been stretched to the limit since 2016. During his campaign and first presidential term, Donald J. Trump became a transparent catalyst for political corruption, crony capitalism, prejudice, and climate change. That break from the cosmetic righteousness of past administrations has made it harder to continue sleepwalking towards catastrophe. People now flock to catastrophe, as though it were salvation, or throw a fit about it, as though it were a personalized insult. Whether enthralled or enraged, we're surely more committed and more polarized than before. But I doubt we're any more conscious.

Dreams of such violent intensity can't last long. It'll all be over in November of 2020, we tell ourselves, or 2024 at the latest. But that's just another coping strategy. Even a clean electoral sweep by the Democrats wouldn't respond to the underlying causes of Trump's rise to power or reverse the long-term effects of his presidency. Awakenings can't be delegated. Plus, Democrats have long been complicit—not in Trump's specific wrongdoings as Republicans have, but in the overall perversion of government that he has stoked and capitalized on.

We won't have all the facts about Trump's presidency for some time. The automatic declassification process doesn't begin until 2045 and the most sensitive government documents won't be made public until 2095.[1] But awareness and power depend more on perspective than they do on data.

This book examines today's democratic crisis from a number of uncommon perspectives, including religion, evolutionary biology, psychology, and even astrophysics. And when it comes to the usual lenses of law, economics, and political science, it applies them to surprising time periods and settings. Why such an unconventional approach? Because, rather than an isolated event, I see Trump's presidency as the natural culmination of our moment in history—especially the parts we've neglected or forgotten.

Celebrating our sins as though they were virtues, he has brought us to the crossroads. Exploiting every weakness, he has pushed democracy to the brink. Rarely has such a portal into the moral, spiritual, and revolutionary dimensions of politics been opened. To all who dare look him in the eye, Trump offers an honest reckoning; and that, I believe, is what the twenty-first century has been asking for all along.

TYRANNY OF GREED

1 A PARABLE

Donald Trump is like an elephant, but I don't mean the GOP's symbolic pachyderm or the one from Ringling Brothers. This Republican creature did turn democracy into a circus, and yet that's not my point. I'm thinking of the proverbial elephant from ancient times. In John Godfrey Saxe's poetic rendition of the parable,

> It was six men of Indostan,
> To learning much inclined,
> Who went to see the Elephant
> (Though all of them were blind),
> That each by observation
> Might satisfy his mind.

The first man runs up against the elephant's side and declares the animal "very like a wall!" The second comes across one of the elephant's tusks and disagrees with the first blind man: no, the animal "is very like a spear!" Encountering the elephant's squirming trunk, the third blind man parts ways with the first two men. No, the

1

animal is "very like a snake!" The fourth man bases his judgment on a massive leg, "very like a tree!" Discovering a large flat ear, the fifth proclaims the elephant "very like a fan!" Finally, the sixth blind man feels the elephant's swinging tail and pronounces the animal "very like a rope!"

> And so these men of Indostan
> Disputed loud and long,
> Each in his own opinion
> Exceeding stiff and strong,
> Though each was partly in the right,
> And all were in the wrong![1]

I fear that historians of the twenty-first century will reach the same judgment about Trump opponents today—over 100 million Americans stumbling around an unfamiliar political regime, trying to satisfy our minds.

Some of us run up against Trump's treatment of women and declare him very like a misogynist! Others come across his promises on trade, manufacturing, and national greatness, and pronounce him very like a populist! A third group encounters the creature's appeal to the alt-right, the violence at his rallies, his views on immigration, his promises to lock up the opposition, and his disregard for legal constraints. You're all wrong, this group says. Trump is very like a white supremacist, an authoritarian, and even a fascist! A fourth band bases its judgment on his emotional instability and need for constant praise. He is very like a mentally deranged narcissist! Discovering the many conflicts between Trump's public responsibilities and private business interests, a fifth group declares the beast very like a plutocrat, an oligarch even! Speaking of oligarchs, a sixth ensemble feels the effects of Russian interference and Trump's loyalty to Vladimir Putin. They pronounce him very like a traitor!

In the parable, the elephant represents God. The blind men represent human beings in search of the divine, declaring our limited experience to be the absolute truth. Can this ancient wisdom shed any light on today's political predicament?

Cautioning against "theologic wars" at the end of his poem, Saxe employed the parable outwardly as social commentary. How senseless and arrogant the religious disputes that consume societies! How futile the conflicts they breed! The lesson for today would seem to be strategic. Instead of succumbing to infighting, the political opposition should accommodate each other's ideas and form a united front.

Though appealing on its surface, that lesson is lethally dangerous. The elephant parable exposes the mismatch between human faculties and the profound reality of the divine. But the political realm is more accessible to our faculties than the ethereal realm. Accordingly, it stands to reason that some people may be right and others wrong. A political leader could actually be a fascist, plutocrat, or traitor, while no elephant is a snake, spear, or fan.

That issue, the proper identification of a political leader, brings us to the potentially lethal part. The parable's time frame is uncertain. If employed to avert a religious war by inspiring humility and brotherhood, then the parable is urgent. Beyond that particular instance, however, the parable doesn't suggest any urgency. Humanity's quest to understand the divine precedes recorded history and is unlikely to ever reach a definitive conclusion. But the situation with Trump—unity versus a surgically precise diagnosis—is more like that impending war. When a critical mass of citizens has failed to recognize fascism, systemic corruption, or treason in time, democracy has been lost, genocides have been carried out, and world wars have been fought. From the fall of Rome to the rise of Stalin, Mussolini, and Hitler, history hasn't allowed much breathing room. Plus, Trump's policies pose a danger beyond anything that history has encountered: If carbon emissions continue on present course, climate change may soon escalate to apocalyptic dimensions. And that's the scientists talking, not the authors of ancient parables.

A final reason for questioning the parable's application relates to factual inconsistencies. Unlike the blind men, Trump opponents have been immersed in dialogue and media reports ever since the 2016 primaries. Consequently, few people assert that Trump is only a sexist, only an authoritarian, only a racist, a narcissist, an oligarch, or a traitor. Trump displays multiple worrisome tendencies and everyone knows it. That clashes with the scenario in Saxe's poem, in which the blind men

> Rail on in utter ignorance
> Of what each other mean;
> And prate about an Elephant
> Not one of them has seen!

Today, Saxe would surely conclude that we rail on in total awareness of what each other mean, and prate about an Elephant we've all seen. Wouldn't he?

By broadening the universe of blind men to include Trump supporters and by delving into the opposition's innermost experience of Trump, we may discover that we're confined within a parable after all. And if we don't come to our senses, the sages of the future will soon be discussing another tragic mismatch between human faculties and an unworldly reality. But will our predicament be understood as a parable about God, just like the one in Saxe's poem?

Donald Trump has long inhabited heavenly palaces, surrounded himself with goddesses, and enjoyed considerable fame. He became the head of the country with the greatest economic and military force—i.e., the most powerful figure in existence. And he has been especially concerned with the territory presently controlled by Israel. So you might joke that ours is indeed a parable about God. But that, in all seriousness, is the line that conservative religious voters were fed.

"God showed up."[2] That's Christian evangelist Franklin Graham explaining the 2016 election. At Trump's inauguration, Graham quoted the New Testament on how we must make "petitions, prayers, intercession and thanksgiving . . . for kings and all those in authority." "Kings" was the key word in that quotation, a reference to a conservative strategy that began on the campaign trail.

Once Trump's adultery and misogynistic comments became too obvious to ignore, GOP megadonor Foster

Friess had a big idea. He could compare Trump to King David. After all, the second King of ancient Israel also kept concubines and committed adultery. Friess wrote a letter reminding his supporters that "all throughout history, God has harnessed imperfect people to fulfil his perfect will."[3] Others—including Jerry Falwell, Sean Hannity, and Secretary of Energy Rick Perry—worked to strengthen the narrative. God had chosen Trump to bring about His will.[4] A film-based revelation of this claim, *The Trump Prophecy*, dramatized the story for mass consumption.

In 2019, Trump indicated that it was all true. Gratefully retweeting Franklin Graham's latest message, Trump broadcasted the idea that he, the forty-fifth president, is comparable to "the King of Israel" and "the second coming of God."[5]

But even if you believe in the possibility of divine intervention in politics, the gravity of Trump's imperfections renders these claims preposterous. Just consider:

- his peculiar gift for insult, ridicule, and the cultivation of hatred;

- his singularly vile comments about women;

- the sex money and hush money he's paid;

- his incessant flaunting of conspicuous wealth;

- his policy of separating immigrant children from their parents and keeping them in cages;

- his racism in elevating fringe figures, such as Stephen Miller and Steve Bannon, to positions of power, and in inviting American congresswomen of color to "go back to their countries";

- his support for violence against protesters at his rallies (offering to pay the perpetrators' legal expenses);

- his unprecedented use of lies, fake news, and foreign powers to deceive voters, divide the nation, and manipulate elections;

- his dependency on foreign agents and influence peddlers—including Paul Manafort, Michael Flynn, Rudy Giuliani, Lev Parnas, and Igor Fruman;

- his camaraderie with dictators and oligarchs— including Vladimir Putin, Kim Jong-un, Narendra Modi, Recep Erdogan, and Rodrigo Duterte;

- his celebration of torture;

- his decision to pardon war criminals and suspected war criminals over the Defense Secretary and Military Secretary's objections;

- and his eagerness to double down on fossil fuels and rescind environmental protections in spite of ongoing extinctions and impending climate chaos.

Pooling such facts, who among us can honestly conclude that Trump is God or an instrument thereof?

The evidence to the contrary suggests an eerie parallel between today's reality and the ancient parable. The blind men's difficulty teaches us about the elusive nature of the divine. But when it comes to making sense out of Trump's rise to power and the government he has established, the difficulty pertains to the elusive nature of depravity instead. Rather than an elephant or God, Americans seem to have stumbled upon the Devil incarnate.

Just bear with me here.

Who else would revel in lawlessness, defile democracy, fraternize with racist and authoritarian leaders, and—as icing on the cake—fornicate with a porn star and a Playboy model? Who else would bring about a political apocalypse? If not the actual incarnation of Satan, Trump would at least appear to be the Antichrist—the end-of-days figure inhabited by Satan. The Old Testament predicts the coming of a persecutor who would "speak great words against the most High and wear out the saints of the most High, and think to change times and laws." The New Testament refers to this figure as the "man of sin" and "son of perdition," the one who would endanger creation by deceiving people through signs and wonders.[6]

This is where a bit of national psychology comes in. On that fateful day in November of 2016, the newspapers declared "Oh My God," "They Said It Couldn't Happen," "Shock and Awe," "House of Horrors." The book about Trump's embrace of the alt-right and Steve Bannon is entitled *The Devil's Bargain*. Then came *Fear* and *The Fire and the Fury*, credible inside views of Trump's White House. In terms of violence to the rule of law, human rights, and the free press, readers can consult *How Democracies Die* and *The Soul of America*.

It's not just subtext: American democracy was the Kingdom of Heaven, Trump is Satan, and the latter has conquered the former. I believe that's the underlying meaning of the "stunning repudiation of the establishment" declared by the *New York Times* on election day. And I believe that's how the political opposition is processing Trump's rise to power, deep down.

Not that many people are publicly comparing Trump to Satan. The Nation of Islam's Louis Farrakhan did so while commemorating the Islamic Revolution in Iran. Comedian Bill Maher did so in an exchange with Ralph Reed, the head of Trump's religious advisory board. Also, police raided the home of a protester who brought a "Trump Is Satan" sign into Republican headquarters in Michigan.[7] So, nothing too credible thus far. Nobody who wants to be taken seriously makes such claims, except for Trump himself, who called Hillary "the devil" several times on the campaign trail and received over 80% of the evangelical vote in 2016.[8] But he's the exception that proves the rule. Most Americans would surely prefer a civil and honest debate.

And that restates the issue. What should you call a person who's the bane of civility's existence and one of the most inflammatory figures in American history? What if, on the merits of their words and deeds, that person really does represent the repudiation of everything holy?

The result is a great deal of psychological stress, whether because of cognitive dissonance or grief. Cognitive dissonance refers to the uncomfortable nature of holding contradictory beliefs such as these:

(A) I live in an advanced democracy and everything's going to be OK; and

(B) the Devil was elected president and is committing savage acts against democracy.

To reduce the discomfort produced by holding these beliefs simultaneously, we might convince ourselves that American democracy was never any good to begin with (change A), limit our negative perceptions of Trump (change B), or swear off all media and political conversations (forget about A and B). These strategies amount to depression and denial, early stages of the grieving process. Anger, another stage in the process, is also commonly observed. Until such psychological reactions are processed and completed, they cause political paralysis, reactivity, and other states of disempowerment.

And that's Trump's strategy—spread the pandemonium far and wide, and then break out another jar from the cabinet. So much chaos and tragedy are rarely served up successively. It's unusual, for example, for someone to lose a parent, then a sibling, and finally a friend in a series of accidents or illnesses. But it's unheard of for such a string of tragedies to continue on and on. Probabilistically speaking, someone suffering that personal doomsday would be caught in a serial killer's vendetta. And they would have no prospect whatsoever for completing the grieving process and moving forward with their life. Grieving processes would be stacked one upon another. Think: catatonic shock.

That's what Trump has achieved in the political context. Human beings' identities and sense of well-being depend on more than just friends and family members. Psychologists have documented that political systems also satisfy a number of vital needs. Democracy, the most important of these systems, consists of a large family of component parts, each of which Trump has targeted for assassination: RIP rule of law; RIP civility and substantive debate; RIP tolerance, equality, and civil rights; RIP policy expertise; RIP public interest and faith in government; RIP alliances, international standing, and global order.

But if the human needs bound up with democracy cease to be met, does that really shake people to their core? You be the judge.

First comes the epistemic need to know and explain the world around us. Democracy provides Americans with a worldview, a set of beliefs and expectations about such essential matters as how power is acquired, exercised, and held accountable. Americans are entirely dependent upon it. It's our mother system. At the same time, democracy is also our most beloved and besieged child. We gave birth to it through the Revolutionary War, extended it through the Civil War, defended it abroad in World War II, and guided it through the Cold War to global dominance. Also, thanks to its victory over such historical evils as monarchy, slavery, fascism, and communism, democracy has also acquired the emotional heft of a savior.

Second comes the existential need to "manage threat and to perceive a safe, reassuring environment."[9] Without that kind of environment, human beings sink into "helplessness and . . . despair."[10] When personal problems put that stability in doubt, people compensate by "placing faith in external systems of control."[11] Economic, religious, and political systems provide different types of reassurances and serve as repositories for different types of faith.

Among political systems, liberal democracy has generally been the most successful at managing such perennial threats as majorities oppressing minorities, minorities oppressing majorities, one part of a government oppressing the other parts, and governments oppressing their citizens. The fall of liberal democracy equals the rise of mortal danger.

Third, social systems satisfy the relational need to "achieve shared reality" with everyone from family members and co-workers to strangers on the street.[12] To the extent we believe in the public good, political legitimacy, and self-authorship in a community of equals, it's there, in democracy, that we come together. Those shared values and worldviews make social interaction mutually affirming. Since the 2016 election season, however, many people have experienced relational disruption from political tribalism. Neighbors have begun avoiding each other. Protesters on the Left have been intimidated and even murdered. Liberals and conservatives now perceive each other as enemies, because their realities no longer permit respect or even toleration of the other.

Though they tend to fly under the radar of conscious awareness, these epistemic, existential, and relational needs are required for well-being. How many of us have processed their loss—democracy's loss—fully enough to come out the other side? They say it takes ten years to process the death of a parent. How long for the death of a nation? Whatever your answer, add a decade or two because our minds are processing the death of the nation at the hands of the political Antichrist, who just so happens to have come to power by popular demand.

Because of this erroneous perception and the powerlessness it entails, we must revisit the parable.

The lesson derived by Saxe is the conventional one, a poetic realization that our limited perceptions of the divine cause theological disputes, when they really ought to cause humility, dialogue, and brotherhood instead. Saxe's Indian contemporary, Ramakrishna Paramahamsa, agreed with this outward lesson, but derived an inward lesson as well. Employing the parable in the esoteric sense, he cautioned his disciples against a limited understanding of God, which would impede their spiritual progress.[13]

What kind of approach to an elephant would someone take if they assumed it was a fan or a rope? Hymns about fans, monuments to ropes, rites and rituals to become more fanlike and ropelike. Ramakrishna feared that if people contented themselves with such limited practices and didn't look more deeply for God, they would never progress. And then those superficial practices might spread, bringing us back to the context for Saxe's reading the parable—entire communities of fan worshippers clashing with entire communities of rope worshippers. Ditto for the wall worshippers, the snake worshippers, the tree worshippers, and spear worshippers. Mass insanity the world over.

Is today's mass hysteria over Trump any more productive? Is our political progress any more satisfactory than the spiritual progress that concerned Ramakrishna?

The problem with the elephant began simply enough, with focusing on highly salient perceptions to the exclusion of the big picture. It's not that those initial perceptions of fan-like and rope-like features were entirely wrong. But even a perfect view of the ears, tail, tusks, sides, trunk, and legs wouldn't reveal how these features enable this kind of creature to satisfy its particular needs within a particular setting. The blind men's fascination with their initial discoveries obscured the truth in all its fullness: they had come across the largest land animal on earth, a collaborative, long-lived pachyderm that thrives in herds led by matriarchs and occupies parts of the Asian and African continents.

It's tempting to think their blindness prevented them from discovering the big picture. Were it not for their visual impairment, these men from Indostan wouldn't have been so reliant on touch—they could have simply taken a few steps back and beheld the greater context. Given their limitations, these men would have had to spend a long time with the elephant in order to understand its nature and its role in the natural world. But surely they could have succeeded over the years by walking and living alongside the elephant. The need for such patient communion would be a wise lesson for any spiritual inquiry. We're all blind in relation to God. That's the inherent predicament of reaching out for the divine from within the material world, attempting to grasp the ethereal with our physical senses.

But when it comes to the worldly task of discovering Trump's nature and his role in the political environment, that predicament shouldn't exist. And yet, something is stopping us from seeing the big picture. The basic context of Trump's species remains hidden in plain sight. Trump has drawn us in too close, just as close as those blind men were to the elephant. His outrageous words and deeds are so palpable, the scatterbrained media coverage so invasive, and the threats to democracy so immediate, that you'd practically have to bend the laws of physics in order to take a step back.

So let's finally own up to our overwhelmed and disempowered state. Americans under Trump might as well be standing in the shoes of John, the Christian prophet, bearing witness to Revelation:

> The dragon stood on the shore of the sea. And I saw a beast coming out of the sea. It had ten horns and seven heads, with ten crowns on its horns, and on each head a blasphemous name . . . The whole world was filled with wonder and followed the beast. People . . . asked, "Who is like the beast? Who can wage war against it?" The beast was given a mouth to utter proud words and blasphemies and to exercise its authority for forty-two months. It opened its mouth to blaspheme God, and to slander his name and his dwelling place and those who live in heaven. It was given power to wage war against God's holy people and to conquer them.[14]

Forty-two months? That's July 20, 2020, almost exactly the length of a presidential term. Who can wage war against the beast? That's the impeachment saga, the Democratic primaries, and the 2020 election in a nutshell. A blasphemous name on each of the beast's seven heads? Sexism, racism, xenophobia, authoritarianism, crass incivility (or pride), corruption, and treason. A war against democracy and its chosen people!

To experience such torment and fear, however, is to be so close to Trump that you can't even see him. Because here's the thing: Trump isn't the Antichrist or Satan, and American democracy wasn't even close to pure prior to his coming. And yet, that overwhelming first impression isn't entirely wrong either. Trump is so worldly that he's otherworldly, so heavily material that he's ethereal, and so natural, in certain urges, that he's practically supernatural; and his uncanny power is bringing about an infernal transformation in society, especially in politics. The problem is, we've mistaken one demon for another.

You may judge me to be another blind man, but I wish to suggest,

Trump is very like Mammon!

That's right, one of the other six Princes of Hell, besides Satan.

2 THE DEMON

According to the Book of Revelation, Satan isn't the only demon with whom we have to contend. When war broke out in heaven, "Michael and his angels fought against the dragon, and the dragon and his angels fought back. But he was not strong enough, and they lost their place in heaven."[1] Note that the dragon isn't a loner—he and his angels fought, lost, and were "hurled to the earth" together.

Revelation specifies that the dragon is the "ancient serpent called the devil, or Satan," but the Bible leaves room for interpretation as to the identity of the other fallen angels. Occupying this space, theologians have offered many classifications of demons, which usually hinge on the sins the demons personify and wield to mislead humanity. In fifteenth- and sixteenth-century writings, for example, Satan is defined by wrath, Lucifer by pride, Asmodeus by lust, and Beelzebub by envy or gluttony.[2]

As the embodiments of different sins, demons make our earthly predicament all the more tangible. In the words of the Gospel of Matthew, "Our Father which art in heaven . . . lead us not into temptation, but deliver us from evil." Those who do the tempting and embody the evils in play may be formidable demons, but, even so, Matthew isn't suggesting that God will do all the work of deliverance himself. People have to do their part by serving God, and in this respect Matthew offers a key piece of advice:

> Lay not up for yourselves treasures upon earth, where moth and rust doth corrupt, and where thieves break through and steal: But lay up for yourselves treasures in heaven, where neither moth nor rust doth corrupt, and where thieves do not break through nor steal: For where your treasure is, there will your heart be also . . . No man can serve two masters: for either he will hate the one, and love the other; or else he will hold to the one, and despise the other. Ye cannot serve God and mammon.[3]

The fifteenth- and sixteenth-century classifications of demons coincide with Matthew on this: Mammon is the demon who represents greed, unbridled greed, the sort that would transform you to the point of loving material wealth and hating God. And so, the Gospel instructs people to choose God and take a stand.

At first, Mammon himself was a god, the ancient Syrian god of riches; but, perhaps on account of budding monotheism, Jesus of Nazareth's antimaterialism, or fighting and falling alongside Satan, Mammon's positive abundance twisted into avarice. The Gospel of Matthew, which appears to have been written in Syria,[4] leaves no doubt: this is no deity to be worshipped, no deity of light. If one's heart resides with earthly treasure, Matthew promises that "thy whole body shall be full of darkness."[5] Pointing towards greed's potential to erase virtues, possess hearts, and enslave minds, this is the kind of description that has been lost in modern times. But ever since the Gospels, that's exactly what Mammon has stood for—the corruptive power of material wealth.

Because of his perfect embodiment of this deadly sin, Mammon earned a place among the Seven Princes of Hell. This is also how he earned a place among the presidents of the United States, but now I'm getting ahead of myself. Before examining Trump's political ascendency, let's step back and take in the big picture. Who is Trump really? What do he and his brand stand for?

Since his college days, Trump has been a businessman. He's been leading the family business, which he renamed the Trump Organization, for over 40 years. By the time he entered the Republican primaries, more than half of Trump's 515 business holdings featured his name.[6] Sixteen years earlier, he explained self-branding to a reporter: "I own a lot of things that I don't have my name on . . . [b]ut when I don't put my name on it, nobody knows that I own it. That's one of the reasons I like putting my name on things."[7]

Many companies are composed of a last name or two, such as Abercrombie & Fitch, but how many of those last names describe the company's goods to a T? Is A&F's casual wear uniquely suited for a "polecat" (Fitch) poised at the "mouth of bendy rivers" (Abercrombie)? But the various meanings of *Trump* describe the man and his products perfectly. It's as though *Trump* were the Latin word selected as the name for his species.

Perched atop skyscrapers, the first of Trump's dictionary definitions are obvious: "a decisive overriding factor" and "an exemplary person." From here, however, things quickly grow more complex. Trump's grandparents' last name was actually Drumpf.[8] They changed it to Trump when they immigrated to the United States. And as for the Trump family symbol, that's a sinister story. Rather than making it up, Donald stole it. The coat of arms displayed by the Trump family on its U.S. properties and merchandise was reportedly taken from Joseph Edward Davies and used to this day without permission.[9] Even the hundreds of millions of dollars that Donald inherited from his father appear to have been acquired through illegal means (in this case, tax fraud).[10] Trump's own for-profit effort to train people in his strategies at Trump University was also plagued by allegations of fraud.[11] (Or perhaps con-artistry was what his students were supposed to learn all along, in which case Trump University delivered.)

Given such reports, Trump's meaning seems much closer to a decisive, overriding factor than an exemplary person. But, thanks to a series of confidential settlements and lengthy court battles, we'll probably never know the truth. The same goes for Trump's apparently numerous extramarital affairs.[12] This coupling of probable wrongdoing with the impossibility of knowing the truth points to an earlier meaning of the word. As a verb in French, *tromper* means "to deceive, to be unfaithful to, to cheat on, to disappoint, [and] to elude."[13] This meaning is still visible in the phrase "trumped-up charges."

Not to be outdone by any other deceitful and unfaithful person, Trump appears to have covered up his extramarital relationships through monetary payments that violated campaign finance law.[14] Similarly, beyond the issues of tax fraud surrounding his inheritance, Trump lied about the amount of that inheritance in order to preserve the false impression that he's a self-made man.[15] He certainly wants others to see him as an exemplary person, but his tactics align with the French meaning, a duplicitous fraudster.

Not all duplicitous fraudsters prevail, however. Some are caught and punished. Others burn out. But not Trump. He succeeded in stealing the coat of arms associated with his name, turning his name into a lucrative brand, and getting away with all manner of unethical conduct along the way to becoming a billionaire and president of the United States. He has even succeeded in running for reelection, despite impeachment (the first president in history to do so). Whether through exemplary characteristics or cheating and deceit, the origin of the word *trump* remains intact, for it is "triumph," nothing more, nothing less.[16] Out of such considerations of power and success, *trump* became the term for "a card of a suit [that] will win over a card that is not of this suit."[17]

Trump's hymns to his own greatness broadcast this essential meaning. He is the sole or primary author of the following books: *Think Big: Make it Happen in Business and Life; Trump: Think Big and Kick Ass; Trump: The Art of the Deal; Trump: The Art of the Comeback; Trump Never Give Up* [*sic*]: *How I Turned my Biggest Challenges into Successes; Donald L. Trump: Think Like a Champion; Trump: Think Like a Billionaire; Trump: The Way to the Top; Trump: Surviving at the Top; Trump 101: The Way to Success; Trump: How to Get Rich*, and, most recently, *Great Again*.[18] His author page at Amazon.com proclaims "Donald J. Trump is the very definition of the American success story, continually setting the standards of excellence." Unabashed, his profile goes on to describe *The Art of the Deal* as "one of the most successful business books of all time."[19] In case you want to absorb the message more deeply still, you can spray yourself with it. Trump's own patented fragrance is called . . . you guessed it, Success.[20]

And that's not all. After dousing yourself with Success, you could drive a Trump classic car to gamble at a Trump casino, then dine at a fancy restaurant in a Trump high rise (accompanied by a Miss Universe contestant if you're successful enough), order a Trump steak, wash it down with Trump water, pay the bill with your income from working at a Trump company (a job you got with your certificate from Trump University), and then go home to a Trump luxury residence where you could catch a rerun of *The Apprentice* before lying down on a Trump mattress and drifting off to sleep while reading *Trump: Think Big and Kick Ass*. Trump has constructed an entire world within our own, one in which everything is bigger, better, and much more exclusive.

But how much of that world is real? Trump's name has marked casinos, resorts, and skyscrapers; yet, he hasn't owned them all. Many have just been branded with his name. Trump did own Miss Universe, Miss USA, and Miss Teen USA for many years; however, his drives proved terribly threatening in the beauty business. He became infamous for pushing sexual attractiveness over intelligence and community engagement, even creeping around the dressing rooms of naked contestants, including underage girls. As he put it to Howard Stern,

> You know, no men are anywhere. And I'm allowed to go in because I'm the owner of the pageant. And therefore I'm inspecting it . . . they're standing there with no clothes. And you see these incredible-looking women. And so I sort of get away with things like that.[21]

This admission is a good companion to his comments about "just kissing beautiful women without waiting" for consent and about how his wealth and fame even give him the power to "grab 'em by the pussy."[22] Trump not only branded women Miss This or Miss That, he also acted like they were his property.

Trump no longer owns the Miss Universe franchise, but his conduct in the beauty business speaks to his feckless relationship with sexual power and desire. It turns out that you can't sell beauty that way unless you're a pimp. A pimp—that's the form that Asmodeus, the demon of lust, might take. After all, demons aren't supposed to be derailed by the sins they embody; they're supposed to spread them. They might also partake in sin and be persecuted for it, but they aren't hamstrung by their own charms. (Others are.) Considering his divorces, his affairs, his struggle to stop his former mistresses from ruining his marriage and political career, and his kid-in-a-candy-store behavior at pageants, it's clear that Trump hasn't mastered lust. He's more like Asmodeus's fool than Asmodeus's chosen one. (Hugh Hefner comes to mind instead.)

Trump has fared far better commodifying material success than physical beauty, proving that he can go "all in" when catering to the wealthy (and to those who wish to appear or become wealthy). Marketing experts have long sold products by associating them with beauty and wealth, as in the bikini model sliding a popsicle into her mouth and the Land Rover parked outside an aristocrat's estate. The companies at issue sell desserts and SUVs, not sex or class privilege, but their customers consume all of it. That's what it means to have a successful brand—that intangible associations motivate people's purchasing behavior, sometimes more so than the pros and cons of the product itself.

Trump has taken this one step further by becoming the brand. He resides in Trump Tower and Mar-a-Lago the way Hefner resided in the Playboy Mansion. I'm sorry to inflict you with this image, but Trump gobbles down steaks like the bikini model wraps her lips around that popsicle. He is to wealth what she is to sex.

Trump sells the image, the stage, and even the accoutrements for wealth, summoning that form of desire and giving it places and objects in which to manifest. That's why some of his residential properties commanded an 80% premium, why some developers would pay a $5 million licensing fee simply to label a tower in Seoul as a Trump Tower, and why some would pay hundreds of thousands of dollars per year to be members of Mar-a-Lago.[23] People at Trump casinos, Trump resorts, Trump golf courses, and Trump residential towers aren't just gambling, vacationing, playing golf, and residing somewhere. They're basking in his light, for Trump is a beacon.

Like the elephant in the parable, he's been out in the open all along: Trump is one of the largest, most conspicuous symbols of greed on earth, an insecure, unethical, and insatiable billionaire who erects gaudy monuments to himself across the continents.

Trump's collection of sinful words and deeds as a political candidate and as president made it natural to jump to conclusions—namely, Trump as Satan or, at minimum, Trump as the Antichrist. The Antichrist is a human being "completely possessed, not by some demon, but by Satan himself."[24] That description raises the question that we should be asking today: What's the name for a human being completely possessed, not by some demon, but by Mammon himself?

A *mammonite* or *mammonist* is archaic English for a person devoted to the pursuit of wealth.[25] At their extreme edge of actual Mammon worship, those terms would be analogous to Satanist. But the Antichrist is a big step beyond a Satanist, and Trump is a big step beyond a mammonist. That step was foreshadowed long ago by something Trump did to the symbol he took from Joseph Davies.

The original Davies family coat of arms consists of an outstretched arm holding an arrow above a shield featuring three lions and two chevrons. At the base of this shield, there unfolds a banner inscribed with the word *Integritas*, "integrity" in Latin. When he stole the Davies coat of arms and began displaying it at his U.S. properties, Donald Trump maintained every detail except one. He erased *Integritas* and replaced it with *Trump*.[26] Or, knowing how Trump's career unfolded, you might say he erased integrity and replaced it with greed.

One day, Trump would carry out the same act of desecration on a much grander scale.

Socrates summed it up early on:

SOCRATES: Surely, when wealth and the wealthy are honored in the city, virtue and the good men are less honorable.

ADEIMANTUS: Plainly.

SOCRATES: Surely, what happens to be honored is practiced, and what is without honor is neglected.[27]

Trump's coat of arms represents this shift. Integritas occupied the portion of the coat of arms that conveyed its motto. As such, it stood as an expression of the family's guiding principle and core belief—their ideal. The symbolic significance of putting Trump in its place was to transform material success and conspicuous wealth into an ideal to be honored.

Ancient Greeks like Socrates understood that different kinds of people conceive of politics in different ways. Lone authoritarian leaders think and act in terms of absolute security. Accountable leaders committed to self-government think and act in terms of freedom, equality, the rule of law, deliberation, transparency, popular responsiveness, and the public interest. They think in terms of civic *virtue* and democratic *integrity*. Only plutocrats, oligarchs, and kleptocrats think and act as though the purpose of politics were moneymaking. These competing mottos or organizing principles would be memorialized in these leaders' respective coats of arms—security, integrity, or money-making. That's why it was so evocative when Trump erased integrity and superimposed his own last name.

Mammon—or someone completely possessed by him—wouldn't be content with the riches he could obtain in business. No, an earthly figure possessed by Mammon would be compelled to expand into politics in order to gain an advantage in the marketplace, twist political outcomes to his favor, and destroy that pesky devotion to civic virtue and democratic integrity, which stands in the way of financial dominion over man and earth. This description doesn't apply to all wealthy people who run for office, however. Prior to 2018, most members of Congress were millionaires in today's dollars,[28] as were most presidents prior to Trump. They have commonly been compromised by their private interests, but in no case has their desire for personal gain risen to Trump's level. Mammonists indeed, but no exorcisms required.

What makes Trump so special within the crowded field of American plutocrats? Just a few pieces of evidence from his 2016 campaign and first year in office suffice to demonstrate a pattern that amounts to a difference in kind.

To begin with, Trump was richer than all previous presidents combined, even controlling for inflation.[29] And he used that wealth to purchase a viable campaign. Few people supported his campaign at first, so Trump spent $66 million of his own money to make his candidacy possible—more money than any other winning candidate in U.S. history ever spent.[30] To supplement these funds, Trump breached his fiduciary duty to his charitable foundation and misappropriated millions of dollars. Some three years after winning the election, he was ordered to pay $2 million to the rightful recipients of those funds as part of a legal settlement.[31] Trump also routed millions of dollars of campaign funds to his own companies for providing staff, hotel rooms, office space, meeting venues, banquet rooms, and air travel, among other goods and services—a process that endured through the 2018 midterms and the runup to 2020.[32]

This self-dealing proves Trump's own prediction in 2000: "It's very possible that I could be the first presidential candidate to run and make money on it," he said.[33]

Lacking political or military experience, another first, Trump ran for office on the platform of his business empire and fame. More accurately, he ran on the force that produced that material success. Here's how he put it on the campaign trail:

> My whole life I've been greedy, greedy, greedy. I've grabbed all the money I could get. I'm so greedy. But now I want

to be greedy for the United States. I want to grab all that money. I'm going to be greedy for the United States. [Applause] It's true.[34]

Trump comes first in all these respects—his wealth, his campaign spending and self-dealing, his lack of any prior experience except business experience, and his frank admission of greed.

Trump's desire to use political power for private gain brings us to another series of firsts. Detailed reports have found an unprecedented number of conflicts of interest at home and abroad arising from the intersection between Trump's businesses and his powers as president.[35] Does he exercise his powers as president to serve his financial interests or the interests of the American people?

For example, given that some of Trump's companies operate in China and their profits depend on the Chinese Communist Party's goodwill, how can we trust that Trump's conduct of foreign affairs is guided by the public interest? When considerations of national security, human rights, or the protection of allies are implicated by Chinese policies, Trump's business interests conflict with the national interest. The same essential question can be asked regarding his dealings with scores of other countries, including Russia. The same question can be asked domestically in terms of Trump's business concerns over tax policy, land use, financial regulations, and interest rates. Who's governing? Trump the businessman or Trump the politician?

Instead of admitting the need to reconcile these two roles, Trump has denied the distinction between them:

"The law's totally on my side, meaning, the president can't have a conflict of interest."[36] That's two statements rolled into one. The first is a legal claim: ethical obligations and legal penalties applicable to other members of the federal government don't apply to the president and, therefore, the president can't technically have a conflict of interest. The second is a philosophical claim about politics: *if prohibitions on conflicts of interest in civil service don't apply to me as president, then there's no reason for me to erect a firewall between my business interests and the political matters within my purview.*

In accordance with these unprecedented views, Trump hasn't released his tax returns or divested himself from his businesses.[37] Instead, he has relied on a revocable trust managed by his older sons. Credible reports suggest that his sons keep him apprised of his companies' affairs and that he may still secretly withdraw funds from the trust at will.[38] Even if Trump does not benefit from the trust while in office, it will be his to claim when his presidency ends. That gives him a considerable incentive for self-dealing. What President Carter did to disentangle himself from his peanut farm President Trump won't do to disentangle himself from a global business empire.[39]

Office of Governmental Ethics Director Walter Shaub resigned his post after "urging . . . Trump to divest from his businesses" in vain.[40] Taking advantage of his power to name the new director, Trump pushed David J. Apol to the front of the line. Apol was already known for compromising the agency's independence and arguing "that the agency is often too rigid in interpreting conflict-of-interest laws."[41] Shaub has since confessed to being "embarrassed" by Trump's conflicts and the appearance of "kleptocracy."[42]

Reacting to this system of government by thieves, over 200 members of Congress filed suit. Their claim alleged that the Trump Organization's foreign business activities serve as an illegal conduit for gifts and benefits—including millions of dollars in payments to Trump by the governments of China, Afghanistan, India, Iraq, Kuwait, Qatar, Malaysia, Saudi Arabia, Slovakia, and Thailand for space in Trump World Tower.[43] The Constitution prohibits federal officeholders from accepting "any present, Emolument, Office, or Title, of any kind whatever, from any . . . foreign state."[44] This Foreign Emoluments Clause was designed to prevent foreign interests from corrupting the judgment of federal officeholders by bestowing them with "any benefit, gain, or advantage, including profits from private market transactions."[45]

Other suits against Trump have invoked the Domestic Emoluments Clause, which prohibits the president from receiving any emolument from the federal government, or state or local governments, besides his official compensation.[46] By frequenting Trump's properties, including his Washington hotel just blocks from the White House, federal and state government officials have arguably increased his compensation and bestowed him with benefits in violation of the Constitution.[47]

Some of these lawsuits have already been dismissed, and others are likely to fail on technical grounds. The Trump Organization has made annual donations to the

U.S. Treasury in an awkward attempt to atone for its foreign government patronage. Still, it refuses to release its tax returns or disclose its foreign clients.

Continuing along in the kleptocrat's playbook, Trump appointed a Gilded Age cabinet worth over $8 billion.[48] Cabinet members shape domestic and foreign policy within the purview of the 15 executive departments. Instead of opting for a strong cabinet with independent expertise or a commitment to the public good, Trump chose people whose personal wealth is tied to the policies they would help formulate. When questioned about this choice, Trump explained, "I want people that made a fortune!"[49]

In many cases, they made their fortunes by undermining the public concerns they're now entrusted with managing. A former coal lobbyist and climate change denier, Scott Pruitt became the head of the Environmental Protection Agency; former Exxon Mobil CEO Rex Tillerson became the secretary of state; Betsy DeVos, a wealthy investor whose family has funded efforts to privatize education, became the secretary of education; Gary Cohn, the president and CEO of Goldman Sachs, became Trump's chief economic adviser and the director of the National Economic Council; Elaine Chao, the daughter of a shipping magnate and wife of the country's number one opponent of campaign finance reform, became transportation secretary;[50] Tom Price, who while serving as a Georgia congressman "purchased shares in a medical device manufacturer days before introducing legislation that would have directly benefited the company,"[51] became Health and Human Services secretary; and Wilbur Ross, a major campaign donor and investor worth an estimated $2.5 billion, became commerce secretary.

Just erase integrity and pencil in greed, and this is what you'll get. Like a coat of arms, the cabinet revealed Trump's organizing principle, which guarantees the alignment of public policy with private profits. This congenital inability to think in ethical terms is the one constant in Trump's life, a quasi-religious devotion to money. Unlike his illiberal populist antics, Trump's corruption doesn't serve to energize his electoral base. There's no political value to it; rather, it's the only really honest thing he does.

Such despicable authenticity brings us back to the heart of the matter: a human being completely possessed by an ancient evil.

If Trump's rise to power is going to be explained, his political regime exposed, and the key to defeating him encountered, then it's time to make eye contact with Mammon. That confrontation requires a courageous level of honesty, because Trump didn't force himself on America. To be sure, he lied, cheated, and manipulated the 2016 election. But those high-profile transgressions haven't dissuaded many of his supporters or the Republican Party. Most observers find both things surprising: Trump's extraordinarily dishonest conduct *and* the decision by a critical mass of insiders and outsiders to stand by him regardless. At the root of this puzzle lies the power of material self-interest in America.

Even at the height of their lascivious empires, would Hugh Hefner or Larry Flynt have been elected president?

Democrats and Republicans have their sex scandals from time to time, but these are never greeted with the attitude that lust is good. As would-be candidates, Hefner and Flynt could never have gained robust political support by stating, *My whole life I've been horny, horny, horny. I've grabbed all the sexual partners I could get. I'm so lustful. But now I want to be lustful for the United States.*

Or maybe I'm giving voters too much credit, but here's what I know for sure. The Marquis de Sade was consistently persecuted for his unbridled lust in the late 1700s and early 1800s, while wealthy landowners ruled Europe and the United States. Hefner and Flynt were leaders of a recent social transformation that surely cost Asmodeus many ill-fated incarnations to achieve.

In contrast, organized greed has played a key role in American democracy no matter how far back you look, from the plantation owners who pulled the strings of Southern governments to the great industrialists who influenced both major political parties for decades. Although slavery was abolished, and many economic and social reforms were enacted to smooth capitalism's roughest edges, the corrupting role of big money in politics was never stamped out. As strange as this might sound, plutocracy actually became the official form of government in the United States just prior to Trump's election.

And so, if there really is a rapacious demon from hell at the heart of American politics today, then there's something we have to face up to:

He was summoned.

3 GENESIS 11:2016

In what kind of democracy could Donald Trump become president? In what kind of America? Judging by the shock and awe surrounding the 2016 election, the answer begins with an admission: it was the kind of democracy we didn't know we had, the kind of America we didn't know we had become.

Compared to other elections, November 2016 was a new world, and every new world has an origin story.

Approximately three quarters of Americans identify as Christian,[1] which means we're accustomed to the origin story involving Adam and Eve. As a patriotic people, we're also accustomed to the origin story that began with the American Revolution and continued through the civil rights movement. However, most of us aren't in the habit of linking these stories. What, after all, could the genesis of earth and humanity have to do with the struggle for democracy? For a nation blindsided by corruption, that's the vital question.

From the Book of Genesis through the rise of neoliberalism, corruption has played a pivotal role in history. And in some of the most influential religious and political texts, corruption has been attributed to demons. This surprising continuity took roughly 300,000 years to sort itself out, but it can be summarized in two parts: the Fall from Eden and the Fall from Democracy.

There, hidden within some of the most important events of all time, lies the backstory to Mammon, Trump, and the country's new postdemocratic era.

PART I: THE FALL FROM EDEN

No sooner do we learn of God creating the heavens and the earth, and get to know our earliest ancestors, than we're confronted with that treacherous snake. In Genesis the serpent tricks Eve into eating the forbidden fruit from the tree of the knowledge of good and evil, Adam joins in, and God punishes them severely. "I will make your pains in childbearing very severe," God says to Eve. (He also declares that her husband will rule over her.) Next, God condemns Adam to a miserable agricultural existence: "painful toil . . . all the days of your life." After being forced to sweat, toil, and eat the plants of the cursed ground, God proclaims that Adam himself will return to that ground, "for dust you are and to dust you will return."[2] Stating that Adam and Eve must not be allowed to take also from the Tree of Life, God banishes them from the Garden of Eden.

Even beyond their gravity, these are no ordinary pun-
ishments, because they apply in perpetuity to Adam and
Eve's offspring. Religious doctrine has long held that subsequent human beings are born into original sin as
though by heredity and must seek out the grace of God
in order to save themselves. This is so despite the fact that
rebellion wasn't Eve or Adam's idea: they were conned by
the serpent.

The third chapter of Genesis warns readers about this
upfront, describing the serpent as "more crafty than any
of the wild animals the Lord God had made." Rather
than revealing his intention to get Adam and Eve to dis-
obey God and eat the forbidden fruit, the serpent asks
Eve a seemingly innocent question: "'Did God really say,
'You must not eat from any tree in the garden?'" That
deceives Eve into thinking the serpent a disinterested
observer with less knowledge than she, when, in reality,
the serpent knows which tree is at issue and harbors a ter-
rible desire. The serpent might reply that he told the
truth about the tree—that the pair wouldn't die if they
ate from it, rather they'd know good and evil. But the
truth or falsity of a particular statement isn't really the
point when it comes to the realization of a sinister plan.
The serpent secretly aims to drive a wedge between God
and human beings, and get them thrown out of their
happy home. That's the first thing that the serpent hides,
because Eve would never trust him if she knew. The other
things the serpent hides are even worse: he's Satan in dis-
guise and he wants humanity for himself.

The events of Genesis—creation, Adam and Eve, their descendants, the flood, the ark, and so on—are so weighty that it's difficult to pause and consider the driving force behind the tragic affair. What caused the fall of mankind to begin with?

Satan didn't force-feed Eve and Adam the forbidden fruit. Rather, he manipulated them in order to maximize his own interests, and he did so at the expense of their most vital interests and those of mankind as a whole. It's the primordial case of the private interest prevailing over the public interest by means of secrecy and deception. And it's also the first case of abuse of power for such purposes, because it turns out that Satan was once an angel, and he employs that celestial power to possess a serpent, thwart God, and manipulate the first humans. To take Genesis at face value is to conclude that corruption caused the fall of mankind and that Satan, foremost among all demons, brought that corruption into being.

But what exactly did Satan con Eve and Adam into doing? I believe the answer is a surprisingly scientific one: Satan conned Adam and Eve into becoming modern humans.

Genesis (2:25) notes that "Adam and his wife were both naked, and they felt no shame." Upon eating the fruit, Genesis (3:6) states that "the eyes of both of them were opened, and they realized they were naked; so they sewed fig leaves together and made coverings for themselves." God said, "Man has now become like one of us, knowing good and evil."[3] He then banished them from the Garden of Eden and declared that Adam must begin working the soil.

In these ways, Genesis points to the emergence of key distinctions between our species and all other members of the animal kingdom: reflective consciousness (giving way to such feelings as shame and modesty), the use of clothing, the cognitive capacity to judge things conceptually (as good or evil, for instance), and the ability to transcend hunting and gathering through agriculture. The curious facts of Genesis reflect a remarkable awareness of what, even back in Christ's time, would have been distant events, events whose only evidence—fossils, tools, cave paintings, and the like—couldn't yet be dated.

Until 2017, our best evidence suggested that human beings emerged in Africa between 200,000 and 260,000 years ago and migrated off the continent around 60,000 years ago.[4] Since then, new fossil evidence has emerged, suggesting that our species is actually much older, at least 300,000 years old,[5] and that some anatomically modern humans left Africa much earlier. Either way, we know that we emerged in Africa at a time when the Sahara was "green and hospitable, a place where antelope and cattle grazed on plants while hippos and crocodiles swam in fish-stocked lakes."[6] That hunter-gatherer paradise was surely the Garden of Eden. From DNA and fossil evidence, scientists are reasonably confident that the first human migrations off the continent ended in death and that *Homo sapiens* today are descended from those who left Africa 60,000 years ago.[7] If that's indeed true, then Genesis is unbelievably accurate.

Around that time, human beings acquired the ability to think conceptually, plan strategically, employ symbols as evidence of distinct beliefs, develop a sophisticated language, retain multiple pieces of information at once, and return to many pieces of information later, at will.[8] Mythology and sophisticated problem-solving abilities would have begun at this point.[9] This cognitive revolution distinguishes modern humans from our ancestors, who were average members of the animal kingdom.

Genesis is probably correct: the migration of our forefathers and mothers away from the Garden of Eden and up to the top of the food chain does appear to have coincided with knowledge of good and evil—that massive software upgrade that ushered in behavioral modernity.

Genesis is also remarkable in its linkage of shame (those fig leaf coverings) and agriculture. When humans began using clothing, some 170,000 years ago, they were responding to Ice Age temperatures.[10] But the emergence of complex clothing, around 40,000 years ago, adds evidence of symbolism and social purpose. And some 30,000 years later, human beings wore loin clothes made of fox pelts, the kind of clothing whose only function was to uphold social norms of modesty.[11] That definitive evidence from 10,000 years ago coincides with the agricultural revolution. That's when hunter-gatherers—for whom the earth was a garden—became primitive farmers. Genesis's account of how Adam felt shame and was then sentenced by God to work the ground accurately links this culturally acquired emotion with agricultural practices.

As a consequence of Adam and Eve's knowledge of good and evil, God banished them and their descendants from the Garden of Eden—a punishment that applied in perpetuity. But why should Adam's and Eve's descendants keep on paying for the crimes of their forbearers? Why should there be any such thing as original sin passed on by heredity to all members of our species?

The reflective consciousness that enables us to ponder our thoughts and behaviors and modify them based on judgment has been passed down genetically to every ordinary human being since. "And the Lord God said, 'Behold, the man is become as one of us, to know good and evil'" (Genesis 3:22). That comparison between *Homo sapiens* and gods announced the newfound ability to transcend animal instincts and the confines of the natural order. Choosing how to live and creating our own social codes (and eventually political systems and civilizations), human beings began authoring our own destinies.

Even if we returned to the site of that original garden, we couldn't reenter it. Genesis refers to the natural order that first contained us, the state of nature that continues to encompass every other animal except *sapiens* and the animals we forcibly exempt—those we domesticate as pets, enslave in factory farms and laboratories, modify genetically, and those that our callous and reckless choices drive to extinction. It seems to me that the angels guarding the gate to the Garden of Eden are in our heads—the parietal lobe and the cerebellum, to be precise. And the proportions of that gate are mirrored by our endocranial size and shape.[12]

Now, let's assume for a moment that the authors and editors of Genesis were actually brilliant ethical teachers, not superstitious weavers of blind conjecture. Let's imagine that they understood that knowledge of good, evil, clothing, and farming was a function of intelligence, not a punishment from some cruel and vindictive figure residing in the sky. Genesis itself, whether written by Moses or P, an Israelite priest from the sixth century BCE, belongs to a larger literature of "creation traditions," all pondering who we are, where we came from, and how we can thrive in society.[13] The biblical mystery then becomes, Why does Genesis attribute the cognitive revolution and behavioral modernity to the Devil—and specifically to corruption, not coercion or force?

Each and every era of recorded history supplies the same clue. Our choices of what to believe, how to behave, and what systems of law and authority to develop have ranged from mass slaughter, rape, subjugation, and empire to egalitarian, self-governing communities based on human dignity. Both modes of life could be observed this century, last century, and 2,000 years ago. But on balance, some form of domination based on pride, superiority, and violence has always tended to gain a foothold. Having lived under brutal regimes, the authors of the Bible knew this only too well. They also knew that behavioral modernity brought about such human mainstays as torture, slavery, and genocide. Our cognitive and behavioral abilities have proven themselves so susceptible to abuse that the Devil might reasonably be blamed for their emergence.

And still, no matter how bad things got, people could always make a choice between love and hatred, compassion and cruelty, generosity and greed, brotherhood and steep hierarchies, forgiveness and vengeance, humility and pride, and honesty and deception—in short, virtue and sin, *good and evil*. Any historical observer could see how one side of these pairings led to suffering and devastation (not to mention, power and riches for the few), while the other side led to happiness and human flourishing. Once the outcome was no longer determined by instinct and the natural order, then morality—and the books of the Bible—became possible. For this one animal species, matters of soul and spirit were suddenly paramount. People were free and vulnerable at the same time. Thus began the high-stakes contest between virtue and corruption.

Satan and Mammon: A Division of Labor

After kicking humankind out of paradise, God reveals himself to be so intent on our redemption and salvation that he sends his own Son to guide us home. But Jesus has to contend with the Devil, who "taking [Jesus] up into a high mountain, showed to him all the kingdoms of the world in a moment of time." The Gospel of Luke notes that Satan offers to make Jesus his deputy: "All this power will I give you, and the glory."[14] Jesus declines Satan's inducement to turn against God and humanity. But that's not the end of it. The Bible doesn't insinuate that Satan made a promise he couldn't keep; apparently, power over the earth is the Devil's and the Devil's to give. The First Epistle of Peter describes Satan as the ruler of the earthly jungle in which we're ensnared: "Be sober, be vigilant; because your adversary the Devil, as a roaring lion, walketh about, seeking whom he may devour."[15]

These passages are pretty bleak. Not only does the Devil con humanity out of Paradise and into an earthly existence of original sin, primitive childbirth, rudimentary farming, patriarchy, and inevitable death, but he also intends to stalk and consume us as his prey. It's here, paradoxically, that Satan's reliance on corruption gives hope. He's not going to physically overpower human beings, force us to be evil, and then feast on our bodies. In literal terms, that would be assault and battery, a nonconsensual surgical procedure called lobotomy, and premeditated cannibalistic homicide. Clearly we must interpret the verb *devour* spiritually, not physically. The Devil represents the dark side of the cognitive revolution. He's the spirit bound up with making the worst behavioral choices, with the abuse of our powers of self-authorship. As we succumb to that spirit, it's as though we're being devoured, for our virtues are gradually consumed by sins.

Sins, plural. That's the cautionary note that ought to be appended to the Fall of Mankind and the Gospel of Peter's warning: the Devil isn't our only adversary nor do his trademark sins have a monopoly on the soul's undoing. The Epistle to the Ephesians stresses the point, cautioning that "we wrestle not against flesh and blood, but against principalities, against powers, against the rulers of the darkness of this world, against spiritual wickedness in high places."[16]

That's the Bible's answer to behavioral modernity. Humility versus pride, honesty versus deception, love versus hate, and generosity versus greed—all those choices are not made at the level of instinct or flesh and blood. Ultimately, such choices are made at the level of spirit and soul, and these, being ethereal, are susceptible to the influence of powers and principalities from beyond.

Among those powers and principalities, Satan's key role is established at the very beginning, with the corruption of our first ancestors. But, the New Testament allows some flexibility in the distribution of labor between Satan and Mammon. Ephesians, above, must be read alongside the Gospel of Matthew's admonition that "Ye cannot serve God and mammon,"[17] which is repeated verbatim in the Gospel of Luke.[18]

Moreover, Jesus's own life and message underscore Mammon's importance. Giving advice to a wealthy man, Jesus says, "You lack one thing; go, sell what you own, and give the money to the poor, and you will have treasure in heaven" (Mark 10:21–25). How Jesus made an example of this man is equally well known:

> Then Jesus looked around and said to his disciples, "How hard it will be for those who have wealth to enter the kingdom of God! . . . It is easier for a camel to go through the eye of a needle than for someone who is rich to enter the kingdom of God."

But Jesus's concern over the corruption of individuals by Mammon was only the beginning.

When Jesus sensed that greed had overtaken the temple where religious pilgrims came to worship and where he gave some of his sermons, he didn't contain himself. The Book of John and the Book of Matthew record Jesus's revolutionary reaction to systemic corruption—in this case, the corruption of religion itself. Here's John's account:

> The Passover of the Jews was near, and Jesus went up to Jerusalem. In the temple he found people selling cattle, sheep, and doves, and the money changers seated at their tables. Making a whip of cords, he drove all of them out of the temple, both the sheep and the cattle. He also poured out the coins of the money changers and overturned their tables. He told those who were selling the doves, "Take these things out of here! Stop making my Father's house a marketplace!"[19]

The Gospel of Mark (11:16) tells how Jesus then instituted an embargo on merchandise traveling through the temple. With some 300,000 to 400,000 pilgrims coming through, this crushed a major source of profit, and those who were profiting from religion would have complained to the Roman or Jewish authorities. If the authorities didn't already have plans for Jesus, they surely drew them up at this point. Within one week of his rebellion against the commercialization of religion, Jesus was dead.[20]

Judas famously helped the chief priests apprehend Jesus in exchange for 30 pieces of silver.[21] Not only is betrayal a classic form of corruption, but this is the most notorious betrayal in history. To explain it, Luke (22:3) and John (13:27) note that "Satan entered" Judas. But would Satan have required any economic compensation for this act? Pride, power, and revenge are his signature motives. Judas's betrayal, on the other hand, was bound up with the spirit of Mammon—and Judas's subsequent regret, involving returning the money before killing himself, was a repudiation thereof.

No matter how crucial Mammon's role, however, the sins associated with Satan tend to be more visible. As the Gospel of Luke states, those intent on Jesus's death accused him of subverting the nation, opposing the payment of taxes to Caesar, and claiming to be a king.[22] That would make Jesus an enemy of the Roman Empire, a dangerous rebel. Crucifixion was, as Reza Aslan notes, "a punishment that Rome reserved almost exclusively for the crime of sedition." Sure enough, the plaque on Jesus's cross read "King of the Jews," for it appeared to the Romans that his "Kingdom of God" was not a place within, but a rival form of political authority whose leader was guilty of insurrection.[23] As far as our classification of demons goes, Jesus's Roman persecutors were moved by pride, insecurity, jealousy, and wrath—the mix between Satan and Lucifer that's commonly lumped together in the form of the Devil.

The same could be said about those who brought the accusations against Jesus to begin with—the chief priests, the teachers of law, and the officers of the temple guard. Pontius Pilate and Herod Antipater, the local rulers of Judea and Galilee under Rome, questioned Jesus personally. Pilate stated to Jesus's accusers and others who had assembled "I have examined him in your presence and have found no basis for your charges . . . Neither has Herod, . . . he has done nothing to deserve death." But the Gospel of Luke records how "the whole crowd" rejected this finding and "shouted, 'Away with this man!'" Apparently not even the teachers of law intervened in support of the judgment exonerating Jesus. Pilate himself appealed to the crowd three times to be reasonable, but they wouldn't accept the rule of law: "Crucify him! Crucify him!" the crowd demanded.[24] Apparently, Satan had entered the crowd, not only Judas.

Such bloodlust also controlled the Roman authorities' reaction to the Jewish Rebellion, which followed some thirty years after Jesus's crucifixion. In response to the "*cruelty and corruption*" of the Romans, Jewish Zealots freed Jerusalem and managed to control it for four years, before an army of 60,000 Romans returned to settle the score. Passing through Galilee, the army killed and enslaved some 100,000 Jews before even reaching Jerusalem. There they "unleashed an orgy of violence[,] butcher[ing] everyone in their path, heaping corpses on the Temple Mount." The city's final moments featured a "river of blood" and then a massive conflagration set by the soldiers.[25] That's Satan in action.

The back and forth between Mammon and Satan becomes dizzying as this period of history draws to a close. At the end of the day, it wasn't just Rome's pride, violence, and expansionist agenda that led to its downfall. Ramsay MacMullen's definitive work *Corruption and the Decline of Rome* summarizes the key factors as "power for sale," "privatizing of public office," "increasing profit from public office," and "the price of privatizing government."[26] This was the same process that Jesus had observed in the temple. But instead of religion, here it was politics and government that became a marketplace.

MacMullen's book exposed how the abuse of power for private gain went from wrongful to normal over time. As economic self-interest replaced reciprocity, debate, and tradition, Rome's laws and policies were distorted and ultimately hijacked. A freed slave from the period noted that such "universal corruption . . . increased the influence of the rich, and aggravated the misfortunes of the poor."[27] Over generations of distrust, Rome's legitimacy declined. After all, it had always depended on popular belief, not just strength and violence. Invasions became more common and harder to repel. Was a marketplace for political power really worth defending?[28] Within a few hundred years of its commercialization of government, Rome was dead.

PART II: THE FALL FROM DEMOCRACY

The gasps and moans of English subjects assembled outside the Palace of Whitehall marked a turning point. The monarch had been decapitated before their very eyes. The year was 1649 and nearly 1,200 years had passed since the last Roman emperor had been deposed. When Roman authorities withdrew from Scotland and Britain in the fourth to fifth centuries AD, numerous kingdoms were drawn up, leading eventually to the British monarchy. But never had a British monarch been put on trial by his own subjects and their representatives in Parliament. Never before had British subjects dipped their handkerchiefs in their ruler's blood.

Charles I had dissolved Parliament multiple times and even waged a series of civil wars against it. After his defeat, Parliament accused him of treason and tyranny in the form of "wicked designs, wars and evil practices." The key element of Charles's crimes is that they were allegedly

> carried on for the advancement and upholding of a personal interest of will, power, and pretended prerogative to himself and his family, against the public interest, common right, liberty, justice, and peace of the people of this nation, by and from whom he was entrusted.[29]

In essence, Charles I's tyranny consisted in the abuse of entrusted power for private gain.[30] That happens to be the leading definition of corruption today.

The High Court of Justice underscored the centrality of corruption in its verdict, declaring Charles I a "public enemy to the good of this nation."[31] He had been "trusted with a limited power to govern by, and according to the law of the land" and "obliged to use the power committed to him for the good and benefit of the people [and] the preservation of their rights and liberties." But instead of practicing a lawful form of rule, the court found that he had pursued "an unlimited and tyrannical power to rule according to his will, and to overthrow the rights and liberties of the people, and to take away and make void the foundations thereof, and of all redress and remedy of misgovernment."[32]

Though Charles I died instantaneously, and Rome declined gradually over hundreds of years, corruption lay at the heart of both affairs. This time around, however, the tables were turned. The people and their political representatives had fought corruption instead of succumbing to it. Abolishing the monarchy and declaring representatives in the House of Commons the source of all legitimate governmental authority, parliamentarians established the first English republic, the Commonwealth.

This was a victory, not a fall. But curiously enough, one of the Commonwealth's best intellectual defenders wrote a book on the Fall. John Milton's *Paradise Lost*, a 12-volume poem, still stands as a powerful rendition of the origin story. Before Milton had finished that work, the Commonwealth requested that he write a rebuttal to Charles I's supposed autobiography. Published after his execution, the *Eikon Basilike* or "Royal Portrait" painted the king as a martyr. Accepting the task of defusing popular support for the restoration of monarchy, Milton wrote *Eikonoklastes*.

Milton's mocking portrait of "His Sacred Majesty in His Solitudes and Sufferings" broke the icon of the King, describing him as a false idol and his followers as idolatrous. *Eikonoklastes* threw the usual accusations at Charles I, including corruption and bribery in his monetary and military policies, opposition to Parliament's role of redressing grievances, and the relentless pursuit of self-interest which led him to dissolve Parliament whenever he couldn't corrupt it. That systematic corruption of mixed government was tyrannical as a political matter, but Milton emphasized Charles's corruption of Christianity as well. He claimed that the people had been convinced of Charles's "zeale, and true righteousness . . . without the pledge and earnest of sutable deeds." Which is to say they had been manipulated or deceived, because "the deepest policy of a Tyrant hath bin ever to counterfet Religious."[33] As a religious counterfeiter, Charles I had manufactured fake righteousness and fake sentiment, conning his followers into worshipping him as a God.

Naturally, their obedience swelled Charles's already considerable pride. *Eikonoklastes* described how the King's obstinacy occurred to him as reason and everyone else's reason occurred to him as faction. In Charles's mind, his title, crown, and unlimited power made him wise by definition, while others' status as subjects made them susceptible to passion and prejudice. On the theory that no earthly authority had the rightful power to judge him, he didn't even defend himself at trial.

And so Milton wrote of one whose "pride had cast him out . . . with all his [supporters] . . . by whose aid aspiring to set himself in glory above his peers, he trusted to have equalled the Most High . . . with ambitious aim . . . raised impious war."[34] This was a figure "mixed with obdurate pride and steadfast hate,"[35] with "vain hopes, vain aims, inordinate desires, blown up with high conceits engendering pride."[36] But these words appeared in the pages of *Paradise Lost*, not *Eikonoklastes*. They are taken from Milton's description of Satan, which brings us to Milton's political genius—his ability to connect the spiritual with the political.

At the start of *Paradise Lost*, Satan and his rebellious comrades are hurled down to "bottomless perdition,"[37] "a dungeon horrible on all sides around as one great furnace flamed . . . torture without end . . . in utter darkness . . . as far removed from God and light of Heaven as from the centre thrice to the utmost pole."[38] Milton calls this place "Chaos" and Satan's palace "Pandemonium." Having waged war in Heaven and been defeated by the Archangel Michael, Satan convenes a great assembly in Pandemonium with his peers and a "thousand Demi-gods" in attendance.[39] There, he and his peers decide whether to wage another war for Heaven, remain in Hell, or set their sights on earth and God's newest experiment, humankind.

Addressing the multitude, Beelzebub counsels his peers against remaining mere Lords of Hell and confining themselves to an empire down below. Reasoning that God made this their dungeon and would rule them even there, he suggests an "easier enterprise" on earth, "the happy seat of some new race called man," which he notes to be like the fallen angels but less powerful, less excellent.

Although Heaven's door may be closed, Beelzebub concludes that earth is vulnerable, and the fallen angels can obtain their revenge by either destroying God's creation or possessing it and its "puny habitants." He thus sets his mind to human beings, wagering that he, Mammon, Satan, and the other fallen angels could

> Seduce them to our party, that their God
> May prove their foe, and with repenting hand
> Abolish his own works.[40]

Interjecting his own voice, Milton marvels at Beelzebub's malicious plan and attributes it partly to Satan, "for whence, but from the author of all ill, could spring so deep a malice, to confound the race of mankind in one root, and Earth with Hell to mingle and involve."[41] Satan's assembly approves, voting to search out and possess this new world and its new race.

Volunteering for the mission and forbidding any other to join him, "Hell's dread emperor . . . the Adversary of God and Man" extends his wings and flies off. Milton then joins his account with Genesis and its narrative of corruption. Describing Satan's choice to possess a serpent, Milton calls the animal a "fit vessel, fittest imp of fraud, in whom to enter, and his dark suggestions hide."[42] Before Satan speaks through the serpent, Milton prefaces those words with "His fraudulent temptation thus began."[43]

Milton is getting at the two dimensions of corruption: individual corruption (that malicious plan to confound human beings) and systemic corruption (the mingling of earth with Hell through the capture of such systems as government and religion). That's what he was describing all along, beginning with Beelzebub's references to the *possession* of mankind as an alternative to mankind's destruction, and the *seduction* of mankind to the demons' party. In order for the Devil to dominate and enslave us, we must be complicit. Demons can't do it on their own. That's what makes the rules of creation—and politics— so fascinating.

Take, for example, the prospect of royalist triumph in the election of 1660. Monarchy, in the gloating figure of Charles II, returned to England via popular choice. If Charles I had really been so insistent on destroying his subjects' liberty for personal gain, why on earth would people wish his son to return and repeat the cycle all over again? It wasn't just that the Commonwealth had performed poorly or that Cromwell had become a tyrant himself, for that republic could be abolished and a new one declared. But the people restored the monarchy instead, which Milton considered not just "a political mistake" but "a moral and spiritual sin."[44] The royalists' desire "to fall back . . . to their once abjur'd and detested thralldom of kingship" was, in Milton's words, "a strange degenerate corruption suddenly spread among us, fitted and prepar'd for new slaverie."[45]

Such corruption and slavery consisted in voluntary subjugation to a ruler, who would "pageant himself up and down . . . among the perpetual bowings and cringings of an abject people, on either side deifying and adoring him."[46] Milton ascribed that voluntary enslavement to "a credulous and hapless herd, begott'n to servility, and inchanted with the[] popular institutes of Tyranny."[47] Being so confounded as to replace the first English republic with the old monarchy, the people had mingled earth with Hell. Essentially, they voted for Satan.

Eikonoklastes makes the same view clear: monarchy was oppressive, prideful, idolatrous, and ultimately disloyal to God. After *Eikonoklastes*, in Milton's last plea for parliamentary government just before the restoration of the monarchy, he describes "Free Commonwealths" as the form of government that has "bin ever counted fittest and properest for civil, virtuous and industrious Nations." He describes monarchy, on the other hand, as "fittest to curb degenerate, corrupt, idle, proud, luxurious people."[48] Virtuous and industrious versus corrupt and idle: here came Milton's answer to the dilemma raised by the fall from Eden, and the need for political systems after that cognitive revolution occurred.

Milton considered monarchy, even under a just king, to be an abdication of God and political responsibility.

> [W]hat madness is it, for them who might manage nobly
> their own affairs themselves, sluggishly and weakly to
> devolve all on a single person . . . not their servant, but their
> lord[,] to hang all our felicity on him, all our safetie, our
> well-being, for which if we were aught else but sluggards or
> babies, we need depend on none but God and our own
> counsels, our own active virtue and industry![49]

Just a few months before the restoration of the monarchy
and his imprisonment for treason against Charles I, Milton offered that spiritual advice about how human beings
should live in political society. Because the Devil can
only enslave souls and mingle earth with Hell by corrupting people, everything depends on how Adam and Eve's
descendants chose to live. Milton's answer is, depend on
God and through self-governance cultivate the virtues.

In the final two books of *Paradise Lost*, the Archangel
Michael takes Adam up a hill. There he tells him of the
events to come, those leading up to the Flood and eventually the Second Coming. When Michael finishes, Adam
replies that he has had his fill of knowledge, he realizes
it was foolish to seek more by tasting the forbidden
fruit, and that the entire ordeal has taught him that it's
best to obey God. There, in what it means to obey God,
Adam imparts his newly acquired sense of how to thrive
on earth:

> [L]ove with fear the only God . . . walk as in his presence . . .
> on him sole depend . . . with good still overcoming evil, and
> by small accomplishing great things, by things deemed weak
> subverting worldly strong . . . that suffering for truth's sake

is fortitude to highest victory, and to the faithful, death the gate of life.[50]

Michael approves of these lessons, but insists that even the sum of all wisdom isn't sufficient for navigating life on earth. Adam must add the deeds that correspond to his new awareness. Michael refers to these deeds as faith, virtue, patience, temperance, love, and charity.[51] Then Michael tells Adam one last thing: if you live this way you shouldn't be reluctant to leave the Paradise of Eden, because "you shalt possess a paradise within thee, happier far."[52] That's the last thing of any substance that Adam hears before descending the hill, collecting Eve, and being escorted out of Paradise.

Milton inserts his prescription of wisdom and deeds at the start of humankind's separation from God and instinct—the exact point at which self-authorship, ideologies, and political systems became possible. In addition to individual integrity, it's a prescription for self-governance and political integrity. Just ask yourself what values and behaviors would make possible a collective journey towards the common good. Just ask yourself how people would have to regard each other in order to live in a community of political equals.

One hundred and one years after his death, Milton's synthesis of religion and republicanism finally found its champions. From King George III's American possessions, a band of colonists declared a revolution against monarchy. "All men are created equal," it proclaimed.

Nobody, not even a king, was any better than anyone else. As for the King's divine right to govern men as his subjects, that was pulverized, for governments henceforth would have to "deriv[e] their just powers from the consent of the governed."

The American revolutionaries swore that the "Creator" had endowed us all with certain rights that could never rightfully be given up or taken away, including "life, liberty, and the pursuit of happiness." Reordering the political universe, they proclaimed that governments existed to guarantee those God-given rights. According to the Declaration of Independence, that was the priority of any legitimate government and the reason for instituting government among men in the first place. Taking this line of thought to its logical conclusion, the Declaration reasoned that "whenever any Form of Government becomes destructive of these ends, it is the Right of the People to alter or to abolish it, and to institute new Government."

The revolutionaries prefaced the Declaration and the war with a sober sense of reclaiming what had been human beings' rightful state all along. It was necessary to assert American independence against Great Britain in order "to assume among the powers of the earth, the separate and equal station to which the Laws of Nature and of Nature's God entitle them." That's the cognitive revolution describing itself. The revolutionaries understood that our innate human capacities allow us to pursue whatever political future—whatever way of living in community— that we wish. To suppress or deny those capacities is to defy God, disrupt the natural order, and oppress human-ity. And so the revolutionaries fought to honor and guar-antee our capacities individually (through rights) and collectively (through representative governance).

As for the sort of ruler who would deny such rights and principles, the Declaration described King George III's character as "marked by every act which may define a Tyrant" and announced that he was "unfit to be the ruler of a free people." Tyranny, then, is the most egregious denial of self-authorship on individual and collective lev-els, what John Locke called "the exercise of power beyond right[,] not for the good of those who are under it, but for [one's] own private, separate advantage."[53] This, or what the Declaration called "absolute Despotism," is the same egregious corruption that Milton observed in Charles I and Satan.

Seeing as how monarchy was thousands of years old and present nearly everywhere, Jefferson and the revolu-tionaries had done much more than defeat a particular monarch. Announcing that the people had the right to be free, as God and the rules of creation had always intended, they broke an age-old enchantment. The habit of servility had been kicked and the strange, degenerate corruption of preferring slavery to self-authorship had been uprooted.

Or so it seemed at first.

Demons Abhor a Vacuum

The spirit of the Revolution endured for a time and to spectacular effect. After defeating monarchy, colonialism, and empire, the spirit of 1776 proceeded to confront other forms of political domination. During the Jacksonian period, white men without property achieved suffrage. Then abolitionists and the North prevailed over slavery. Constitutional amendments to ensure abolition, due process, equal protection, and African American suffrage followed on the Civil War's heels. Some forty years later, another string of revolutionary accomplishments ensued with the Seventeenth Amendment's provision for the popular election of senators, the Nineteenth Amendment's establishment of female suffrage, and congressional legislation giving Native Americans and Chinese immigrants a path to citizenship and suffrage. By the early 1940s, the country had confronted political exclusion on the basis of property ownership, race, religion, sex, and ethnicity. The popular sovereignty and political equality proclaimed by the Declaration of Independence became a realistic possibility for the first time.

In the same decade, Americans finally got a full view of political evil in the forms of Nazism and Fascism. After helping to eliminate those systems, the nation set its sights on another political system that amounted to domination—Soviet communism. But those external threats didn't stop the ongoing democratic revolution at home. During the Cold War, the civil rights movement

finally forced the nation to confront the injustices that
continued even after African American suffrage—which
included segregation, poll taxes, literacy tests, and white-
only primaries. After the passage of the Twenty-Fourth
Amendment (abolishing poll taxes), the Civil Rights Act,
and the Voting Rights Act, everyone could finally claim
rights of freedom, equality, and self-governance. With
the enforcement of these laws in the early 1970s, democracy began in earnest. And then, less than two decades
later, the United States achieved global supremacy with
the fall of communism.

Having defeated political exclusion and domination of
so many varieties, the democratic spirit rested. Couldn't
it safely do so at last? Had he lived to see popular sovereignty and political equality advance so far, Milton might
have declared that Satan's political hierarchies had finally
been forced back down to Hell. It can hardly be denied:
Dorr's Rebellion, abolitionists, suffragettes, and Martin
Luther King Jr.'s march on Washington all reflected the
power of Adam's lessons in *Paradise Lost*. Pro-democracy
movements walked as though in God's presence, with
good still overcoming evil, and by small accomplishing
great things, by things deemed weak subverting worldly
strong, showing that suffering for truth's sake is fortitude
to highest victory, and for the faithful, justice and democracy their reward. If the deeds behind these movements
were not marked by so much faith, virtue, patience, temperance, love, and charity, universal suffrage would have

never been achieved and official forms of discrimination would never have been abolished.

But was American history from 1776 to the early 1970s really so linear and progressive? From the standpoint of Satan's sins, the obdurate pride and steadfast hate emphasized by Milton, there's a good argument to this effect. Political exclusion on the basis of royal birth, race, religion, ethnicity, and sex had been eliminated, or at least prohibited. People could not be lawfully dominated along these lines. So much for superiority, pride, and hate as the foundation of government.

On the surface of things, these sins appeared to be the prime motivations for American history's worst evils. Take, for example, the slave republic of propertied white men who ruled with whips and chains. Plantation owners and their allies saw blacks as "beings of an inferior order [who] might justly and lawfully be reduced to slavery for [their own] benefit." That's how the Supreme Court put it in 1857.[54]

Or recall the industrial republic of corporate trusts and robber barons enriching themselves off child labor, union busting, and homicidal job conditions. The great industrialists saw themselves as superior to the average Americans who languished in sweat shops, such that they could "recogniz[e] as legitimate those inequalities of fortune" that accrued during the time.[55] Those are the Supreme Court's words from a 1915 opinion, striking down a law that constrained employers' tactics against union membership.

Slavery and the excesses of industrial capitalism were both justified as the inevitable outcomes of a natural hierarchy, much like the steep pyramid that separated the peasants and the nobility of old.

But just a few inches below the surface, Mammon's sins, not Satan's, animated slavery and unregulated capitalism. In his remarks on the corruption of America by "the slave power," Senator Henry Wilson homed in on the plantation owners' domination of government, not just their domination of human beings.[56] That's what the Confederacy was, government by plantation owners for purposes of profit maximization. As the Reverend Henry Ward Beecher put it, this "plutocracy" of wealthy white supremacists held "disproportioned political power" and was "dangerous beyond anything that the mind can conceive."[57]

Congressman Milford W. Howard offered a similar diagnosis for the evils of the industrial era. He began by noting that the laws in force at the time obligated "a vast army of people . . . to labor and toil in poverty in order that the few . . . may lead lives of idleness and luxury."[58] Howard then located the underlying cause of these arrangements in the political parties that "go to the money power for campaign funds, and put themselves under obligation to plutocracy at the very outset."[59] Or as Senator Richard Pettigrew put it, "[T]he few men who own nearly all the wealth have gained control of the machinery of public life[,] . . . usurped the functions of government and established a plutocracy."[60]

In these formidable works, the great injustices of the time were mainly a function of greed, with pride and hatred as mere adjuncts.

Other statesmen conveyed greed's threat to democracy in terms that summoned to mind the greatest threats of old. To reflect upon Thomas Jefferson's phrase, an "aristocracy founded on banking institutions and moneyed incorporations," Martin Van Buren's, "moneyed oligarchy,"[61] and Franklin Delano Roosevelt's "economic royalists," is to picture Mammon digging up the corpses of past power structures and resurrecting them. FDR also referred to the inequality of his day as "economic slavery" and the "new despotism."[62]

Such phrases indicate that Satan had passed the baton to Mammon, a possibility which was there all along in Locke. After defining tyranny in terms of the abuse of power for private, separate advantage, Locke wrote that it was "a mistake[] to think this fault is proper only to monarchies." He noted that "other forms of government are liable to it, as well . . . [f]or wherever the power is put in any hands for the government of the people, and . . . is . . . made use of to impoverish, harass or subdue them . . . There it presently becomes *Tyranny*."[63]

The trouble is that, unlike monarchy or slavery, plutocracy proved itself a recurrent tyranny in America. It impoverished, harassed, and subdued Americans throughout the entire antebellum era. It was then reincarnated during the Industrial Revolution, lasting through the

1930s. The Civil War strangled the slave plutocracy and the New Deal gradually defused the industrial plutocracy, but they did so without actually ruling out class government forever more. There was no war or revolution against government by and for the wealthy, no constitutional amendment or series of enactments to prevent the undue influence of concentrated capital over political parties, elections, law, and policy.

Finally, after the civil rights movement successfully confronted segregation and enduring discrimination on the basis of race and sex, the time came to revisit the tyranny of greed. Once civil rights legislation had been enforced, John Rawls turned to money in politics, writing that

> The Constitution must take steps to enhance the value of the equal rights of participation for all members of society . . . Those similarly endowed and motivated should have roughly the same chance of attaining positions of political authority irrespective of their economic and social class . . . [L]iberties . . . lose much of their value whenever those who have greater private means are permitted to use their advantages to control the course of public debate.[64]

Rawls's concerns became more salient after the Watergate scandal, and in 1974 Congress finally passed the nation's first comprehensive campaign finance reform act.

Limiting political donations and expenditures in all federal campaigns, Congress sought to fulfil three purposes: first, to "prevent[]corruption and the appearance of corruption"; second, to "[e]qualize the relative ability of all citizens to affect the outcome of elections"; and, third, to slow "the skyrocketing cost of political campaigns, thereby . . . open[ing] the political system more widely to candidates without access to sources of large amounts of money."[65] In addition to limits on money in politics, Congress provided for some public financing of elections and an agency to interpret and enforce the new rules. Many states also implemented safeguards against plutocracy.

For the first time in American history, democracy was on the verge of consolidation, with the most significant grounds for political exclusion and domination being abolished—race, religion, sex, ethnicity, and, at last, socioeconomic status. The political branches weren't the only ones that could exercise powers of government, however.

In Washington, D.C., a marble temple stands first among all buildings on First Street. Beyond its pillared façades, through its 13-ton bronze doors, past its Great Hall, and before an enormous red velvet curtain, sit nine figures clad in black robes—the high priests and priestesses of justice appointed for life to interpret the nation's holy document, the Constitution.

This temple is supposed to be democracy's house, but it has proven itself vulnerable to other influences. In 1905, five of its justices legitimated the unregulated labor conditions of the industrial era, affirming that business owners' right to insist on unlimited work days in employment contracts was part of the liberty protected by the Fourteenth Amendment. The Fourteenth Amendment was passed after the Civil War to protect freed slaves from racist state actors who would deny them due process of law. It was cruelly ironic, therefore, when the justices used it to sustain the new economic slavery of the industrial era instead. On such occasions, they used the Constitution as a free-market enforcement device. But they had yet to convert the unregulated marketplace into a system of political rule.

The Supreme Court took that final step in 1976, as though the nation's bicentennial were a fitting occasion on which to declare the birth of a new form of government. The majority opinion in *Buckley v. Valeo* determined the constitutionality of Congress's comprehensive campaign finance legislation. As for Congress's goal of slowing the rise of money in politics, the view from the temple was defiant. The justices defined "the free society ordained by our Constitution" as one in which "it is not the government, but the people . . . who must retain control over the quantity and range of debate . . . in a political campaign." Congress had limited money, not speech, much less any particular content or viewpoint; but in the vision of government that emerged from the temple, political spending was free speech protected by the First Amendment. And unlimited spending was democratic flourishing, not class government.

As for Congress's interest in equalizing citizens' ability to affect the outcome of elections and opening elections to those without significant wealth, the justices saw the opportunity to end the centuries-long evolution towards political equality:

[T]he concept that government may restrict the speech of some elements of our society in order to enhance the relative voice of others is wholly foreign to the First Amendment, which was designed to secure the widest possible dissemination of information from diverse and antagonistic sources.[66]

There was an irony in this imposition of an open marketplace for political spending. Milton's political legacy had been appropriated for the realization of a purpose he'd detest.

Milton's mid-seventeenth-century political writings joined in a current of voices, announcing that the monarchy's control of the press was an affront to God. As the subtitle of John Goodwin's 1644 work, *Theomachia*, put it, the issue was "The Grand imprudence of men, running the hazard of Fighting Against God, in suppressing any Way, Doctrine, or Practice."[67] Such works laid the groundwork for liberal democracy by positing that truth would prevail over falsehood by God's grace, so long as the playing field were level, so long as all voices could be heard. "All mens mouthes should be open," stated William Walwyn, "so errour may discover its foulness and trueth become more glorious by a victorious conquest after a fight in open field."[68]

It was this venue (the open field), this struggle (the fair fight), and this holy force (the truth) that inspired believers to agitate for free speech. Of truth, Milton wrote "Let her and falsehood grapple," for "who ever knew truth put to the wors, in a free and open encounter?"[69] Without the monarch's censorship and coercion, people might govern themselves virtuously.

How could the justices see limits on money in politics in those same terms—the monarch's censorship and coercion? Congress had targeted no particular party or viewpoint, only the ability to make one's viewpoint disproportionately powerful through wealth. Congress had limited political spending, not eliminated it—there was no coercion here, only the maintenance of a reasonably level playing field, the fair fight that believers in truth had always relished. And the government enacting these measures wasn't the hereditary monarchy that Milton, Goodwin, and Walwyn opposed. Nonetheless, the justices treated popular limits on the financial aristocracy with the same hostility as Milton treated aristocratic attacks on the republic. Which is to say, Milton opposed political domination by prideful royals, while the Supreme Court ensured political domination by greedy oligarchs.

But Milton and the high priests of justice did have one thing in common: they both had absolute faith in sacred forces that would sort out political affairs, if only people would just get out of the way. For Milton, those forces were virtue and God. For the justices, those forces were self-interest and the unregulated marketplace, conjured up as principles of constitutional law. The First Amendment was enlisted in the service of greed instead of truth. But there was no zealot around—like Jesus of Nazareth—to turn over the law books, berate the justices, and drive them out for turning democracy's house into a marketplace.

The long trajectories of monarchy and theocracy had indeed ended, but the reign of plutocracy had officially begun.

Had Milton witnessed this counterrevolution against democracy, he would have surely revised *Paradise Lost*. Before Satan's consult begins, Milton introduces us to Mammon who, heading up a brigade armed with spades and pickaxes, is tearing into one of Chaos's hillsides to extract "ribs of gold" from the ground. Milton calls him the "least erected spirit that fell from Heaven," because even there "his looks and thoughts were always downward bent, admiring more the riches of Heaven's pavement, trodden gold, than aught, divine or holy, else enjoyed in vision beatifick."[70] Nothing besides riches ever inspired bliss in Mammon.

Addressing Satan, the rest of his peers, and the multitude of evil spirits in attendance at the great consult, Mammon reasons that if God should allow them to regain their place in Heaven this would be worse than Hell, for their days would thereafter consist of "strict laws . . . warbled hymns . . . forced halleluiahs [and] servile offerings." Urging a different course instead, Mammon summarizes American revolutionary thought in eerie precision:

> Let us . . . seek
> Our own good from ourselves, and from our own
> Live to ourselves, though in this vast recess,
> Free, and to none accountable, preferring
> Hard liberty before the easy yoke
> Of servile pomp. Our greatness will appear
> Then most conspicuous, when great things of small,
> Useful of hurtful, prosperous of adverse,
> We can create;[71]

But then Mammon's plea for self-governance takes a darker turn:

> Our torments also may in length of time
> Become our elements; these piercing fires
> As soft as now severe, our temper changed
> Into their temper . . . how in safety best we may
> Compose our present evils[.][72]

In Milton's work, Mammon's wicked form of self-governance would be confined to Hell. It's Satan who journeys up, orchestrates the fall from Eden, and then proceeds to dominate mankind.

The role of greed in the events surrounding Jesus and Rome ought to have given Milton pause. But I like to think that the slave plutocracy, the industrial plutocracy, and the *Buckley* opinion would have caused him to issue a revised American edition of *Paradise Lost*. Falling for Mammon's ploy to subjugate the political sphere to the economic sphere, the Supreme Court forced the nation out of democracy's garden and down to plutocracy's desert soil, where—during the decline of Rome, the antebellum South, and the Gilded Age—Mammon had been composing his evils all along.

Looking back on how things have gone since the 1970s, it's apparent that Mammon did more than cause the fall from democracy. He turned *Homo sapiens* into *Homo economicus*.

4 MAMMON FOR PRESIDENT

Humans are nothing if not adaptable. *Homo erectus* learned to walk upright; *Homo habilis* invented tools; *Homo neanderthalensis* adjusted to cold climates; and *Homo sapiens* learned to cooperate in large numbers on the basis of symbols and shared beliefs. Those beliefs have varied significantly throughout history, including animistic forces, polytheistic and monotheistic religions, the divine right of kings, and even pseudoscientific ethnic hierarchies of a genocidal persuasion. Our adaptiveness to religious, economic, and political systems easily surpasses our adaptiveness to ecosystems. From Enron traders to Islamic terrorists, people act out the ideology that rules the hive mind—and it doesn't hurt if there are million-dollar bonuses or 72 virgins to be gained.[1]

Knowing this about the species, you might expect that people would adapt to the political marketplace imposed by the Supreme Court in 1976. And so we did. Soon enough, the average successful campaign would require over $1 billion on its side to win the presidency, $15 million for a Senate seat, and $1.5 million for the House. And, in all congressional elections from 2000 to 2018, the candidate who had raised the most money would be elected over 80% of the time.[2] These statistics wouldn't matter as much if all citizens could afford to provide their preferred candidates and parties with substantial monetary support; but they can't, and those who can are unrepresentative of the general public.

That undemocratic foundation raises the salient issue, because throughout history a minority of human beings has generally dominated the majority in the service of an ideology. The uncertain parts are, Which human beings will exercise control? In the service of which ideology? And where will they take the nation?

In the absence of limits on how much candidates, parties, and citizens could raise or spend to affect electoral outcomes, politicians and wealthy interest groups developed a symbiotic relationship. The organisms most successful at raising money and the organisms most successful at supplying that money flourished, while others died off. In this political ecosystem, the mechanism that improves one's chances of obtaining political power isn't an inherited trait; it's a learned behavior called corruption—in particular, the legal, first-world sort of corruption that the Supreme Court justified between 1976 and 2014.

Over this 38-year trajectory, worldviews and power relationships shifted in favor of concentrated capital.

American voters were transported to a place where Donald Trump became not only viable as a candidate, but inevitable as a political force.

A JOURNEY TO THE FAR REACHES

In order to mount a viable campaign for public office, candidates must appeal to political investors, speculators in the market for political futures. In 2016, for example, just 158 families provided nearly half of the seed money for all nascent presidential campaigns, giving more than $250,000 each on average. Another group of 100 families gave over $100,000 each.[3] By the time the election cycle was over, 0.66% of the adult population had supplied 70% of all federal campaign funds.[4] And that was actually an unusually democratic figure, because, expanding the data set, a mere 0.36% of the adult population stood behind the great majority of campaign donations from 1990 onwards.[5]

In addition to comprising a very small percentage of the general population, the donors who've captured the privatized market for viable campaigns represent an exclusive demographic. Studies suggest that they're 99% white, 70% male, mostly 45 years of age or older, and, obviously, much wealthier than most Americans.[6] And yet, even if you lumped all older, wealthy white males together, you still wouldn't have a good picture of the donor class. Its signature trait is the least tangible of them all, a worldview.[7] Following a conservative economic ideology, the most significant cohort of the donor class supports tax cuts, austerity measures, and privatization.[8] It opposes public education, unions, collective bargaining, universal health care, and a living wage.

The disproportionate power of this unrepresentative class of people raises obvious concerns for political participation, government responsiveness, and representation. One simple phrase describes the ability of donors and spenders to filter out unacceptable candidacies at the start and decide the economic power of all viable parties and campaigns up until the moment of the vote: financial aristocracy. This was precisely the class-based system of corrupt government that Congress sought to abolish in 1974. With campaign expenditures capped by law, candidates would have no incentive to fundraise beyond a certain reasonable point. Those who continued dialing for dollars and hosting $10,000 per-plate dinners wouldn't be able to use the funds, gaining no further advantage over their rivals. In fact, they'd fall behind other candidates who were busy holding rallies, meeting ordinary constituents, and searching for popular solutions to public policy issues.

By denying government the power to protect integrity, equality, and the rights of those who can't afford to purchase access and influence, the *Buckley v. Valeo* decision guaranteed a race to the bottom. Candidates, officeholders, and parties faced a choice: maximize and reward financial support or fall behind those who do so. Businessmen, interest groups, and corporations faced a similar choice: maximize political access and influence or fall behind those who do so.

Naturally, *Homo sapiens'* adaptive abilities took off. Candidates and officeholders began spending roughly half of their time fundraising. Officeholders from both parties gave speeches ghost-written by lobbyists.[9] Corporations donated millions of dollars to a group that brought business leaders and political representatives together to develop model bills—actual private interest legislation. Thousands of these bills were introduced by state legislatures and nearly 20% of them were enacted into law.[10] And these are just a few examples amidst a sea of corruption. As unscrupulous political actors obtained advantages over and over again, an evolutionary outcome obtained: conscience became self-eliminating.

Opposing these ongoing alterations to the political genome, state and federal lawmakers passed a variety of additional regulations on money in politics, including public financing systems, limitations on corporate political spending, and limits on contributions and expenditures. Their goals included protecting the time of elected officeholders so they could focus on public service instead of fundraising, combatting the undue influence of concentrated wealth, allowing candidates of humble means to compete against wealthy, self-financing candidates, and protecting democratic integrity and popular sovereignty. Because the Constitution is silent on all matters of money in politics, the fate of these laws turned on the ideologies of the high priests and priestesses of justice.

When monied interests brought suit, the robed figures channeled the commands of their higher power.

Sometimes the high priests wrote so transparently that their prose became farcical. A 2008 case, *Davis v. FEC*, comes to mind. Justice Alito's majority opinion struck down a rule allowing candidates to raise additional funds from their party and donors when an opponent spent over $350,000 of their own money. Here's the reasoning:

> Different candidates have different strengths. Some are wealthy; others have wealthy supporters who are willing to make large contributions. Some are celebrities; some have the benefit of a well-known family name. Levelling electoral opportunities means making and implementing judgments about which strengths should be permitted to contribute to the outcome of an election. The Constitution, however, confers upon voters, not Congress, the power to choose.[11]

That was Alito's entire list of strengths. He didn't include a single civic rationale for electoral choice, such as integrity, views on the merits of policy issues, or political record. Beyond omitting civic strengths, the ruling stopped citizens from acting collectively, through government, to ensure that such strengths remained relevant despite the relentless flow of private wealth into the political process.

Mammon's design for self-governance can also be seen in *Citizens United v. FEC*. The court had long upheld limits on corporate electioneering on the basis that they combatted the undue influence of concentrated wealth.

But Justice Kennedy's majority opinion stated that this democratic purpose "interferes with the 'open marketplace' of ideas protected by the First Amendment." Here, farce would meet dystopia.

Noting that "[a]ll speakers . . . use money amassed from the economic marketplace to fund their speech," Kennedy considered that "[i]t is irrelevant . . . that corporate funds may 'have little or no correlation to the public's support for the corporation's political ideas.'" Flatly contradicting bedrock principles of political morality and civic virtue, his opinion protected plutocracy: "That [monied] speakers may have influence over or access to elected officials does not mean that these officials are corrupt."[12] Political integrity, then, entails a state of affairs in which the market-determined level of money in politics freely conveys the merits and demerits of any candidate or idea, and determines their power.

The practical impact of this economic freedom soon became clear. Unlimited expenditure groups called super PACs emerged, amplifying the voices of an even smaller, more exclusive group than the donor class described above. For example, 80% of the $1.1 billion in outside spending during the 2012 elections came from approximately 200 donors—just 0.000084% of the adult population.[13] In the 2014 elections, two thirds of the $90 million raised by the liberal Senate Majority PAC and the conservative American Crossroads PAC came via donations of $500,000 or more.[14]

Beyond controlling the market for political donations and expenditures, a tiny aristocracy of wealth also controls the market for paid intermediaries who provide biased information to officeholders. That too is the culmination of an evolutionary process. Payments to lobbying firms more than doubled between 1998 and 2010. Rising from $1.44 billion to $3.47 billion,[15] those investments reached the point at which corporate lobbyists outnumbered state and federal officeholders, and the budget for corporate lobbying exceeded Congress's own operational budget by a wide margin.[16] By 2012, business groups were spending 34 times more money on lobbyists than public interest groups and unions.[17] By 2014, it was public knowledge that politically active corporations gained $4.4 trillion in federal support through lobbying and political spending—a 560% return on their investment.[18]

Those who created this ecosystem and those who adapted to it share essentially the same ideological and behavioral traits, those of the self-interested profit maximizers known as *Homo economicus*. The nation's trajectory through political space-time caused this breed of candidate, officeholder, constituent, party, and interest group to flourish.

Opinion polls over the decades show that the general public has had its eyes open on the journey. By the late 1990s, surveys suggested that 77% of Americans believed that "elected officials in Washington are mostly influenced by the pressure they receive on issues from major campaign contributors;" 76% believed that "Congress is largely owned by special-interest groups;" 71% agreed that "[m]oney makes elected officials not care what average citizens think;" and only 19% believed that officials are most influenced by the "best interests of the country."[19]

In April of 2014, the announcement finally came. The country had arrived at the point in the political universe designated by the high priests of Mammon. This point had four dimensions: (1) the official union of corruption and democracy, (2) a corresponding level of political inequality, (3) a corresponding level of economic inequality, and (4) the public's psychological reaction to all of the above. All four were exposed by nearly simultaneous publications, which I call the April Revelations.

On April 2, the Supreme Court struck down a $123,200 limit on total campaign donations per individual donor in each election cycle.[20] By overturning this part of Congress's comprehensive post-Watergate reforms, the majority opinion in *McCutcheon v. FEC* reopened the political process to donors who wished to give millions of dollars to political parties and candidates. The court conceded that large political donations buy "ingratiation and access" to politicians, but held that this didn't justify limiting donations. Beyond deciding that "ingratiation and access are . . . not corruption," the majority opinion insisted that ingratiation and access on the basis of large donations "embody a central feature of democracy." That central feature was simple: donors and spenders "support candidates who share their beliefs and interests and candidates who are elected can be expected to be responsive to those concerns."[21] Warped by the Roberts Court, the Constitution now views political responsiveness to wealth as democratic, not corrupt. A mere seven days later, definitive evidence confirmed this was how American democracy actually worked.

On April 9, political scientists Martin Gilens and Benjamin Page published an analysis of policy outcomes across nearly 2,000 issue areas at the federal level.[22] Their findings showed that "economic elites and organized groups representing business interests have substantial independent impacts" over U.S. government policy, while "mass-based interest groups and average citizens have little or no independent influence."[23]

Gilens and Page pointed to a handful of causes for such extreme political inequality, including pro-wealth biases in campaign finance, lobbying, and the revolving door between public and private employment.[24] To discover how such extreme political inequality affected the distribution of wealth, the nation only had to wait six days.

Published in English on April 15, Thomas Piketty's *Capital in the 21st Century* demonstrated that the United States had become the most economically unequal of all advanced democracies. After 40 years of rising inequality, the top 10% of U.S. wealth holders had finally captured over 70% of all national wealth. Meanwhile, the poorest 50%—150 million Americans together—had been reduced to owning just 2% of national wealth.[25]

This distribution of wealth from 2010 harkens back to the era of child labor and sweatshops, the slavery era, and even feudalism.[26] Surveying historical comparisons, Piketty harped on the fact that inequality of such magnitude isn't natural, even within capitalist economies; rather, it's a political phenomenon, the product of laws and policies that have privatized public resources, deregulated industries and markets, favored capital over labor in the tax code and constitutional rights, favored high-wage earners over the rest, and downgraded social programs and safety nets.[27]

It was a bleaks picture: the most economically unequal of all advanced capitalist nations, ordinary Americans having essentially no political influence whatsoever, and a decision from the nations' highest court indicating that this is how democracy is supposed to work. The kind of capitalism, democracy, and constitutionalism that Americans had believed in and depended on was officially over. But it wasn't clear whether people would tolerate such an unequal status quo. That evidence rolled in just one week later, a fourth revelation.

On April 22, psychologists published the results of experiments on acceptance of authority under conditions of increasing powerlessness.[28] Those conditions included disadvantages stemming from the economic system, government discrimination, and socioeconomic standing. The question was, How would people react to the authorities and social systems that were responsible for extreme inequality? For now, let's just say that the findings were off the charts.

By the time the 2016 election rolled around, American democracy had reached a point in the political universe that used to be impossibly distant. There, at that remote location, it came within the gravitational field of a super-massive force.

THE EVENT HORIZON, 2016

What exactly pulled the nation further, to the point of no return? A combination of factors led to democracy's disintegration and Trump's triumph, and most were in place well before the vote.

The first factor allowed Trump to win the election despite losing the popular vote by 2,864,974 votes and receiving the support of little more than 25% of registered voters nationwide. The Electoral College, that indirect, state-based system of electing the president, doesn't usually defy the popular will. After Andrew Jackson in 1824, Samuel Tilden in 1876, Grover Cleveland in 1888, and Al Gore in 2000, Hillary Clinton was the fifth candidate to win the popular vote yet lose the presidency. From the standpoint of the right to have one's vote counted and the legitimacy of a system based on popular consent, there's something inherently corrupt about the national leader coming to power in spite of a nearly three million vote deficit.

Still, the Electoral College is written into the Constitution. Going into the election season, Clinton and Trump both knew that some combination of Michigan, Wisconsin, Pennsylvania, Florida, and Ohio would likely prove decisive. Winning these and several other narrowly contested states, Trump prevailed by a 14% margin in the Electoral College (306 to 232 electoral votes, subject to a few defections). That sizeable victory is misleading, however. Because most states allocate their votes on a winner-take-all basis, Trump obtained that initial 14% electoral advantage by miniscule margins of victory in Michigan, Wisconsin, Pennsylvania, and Florida. On average, less than 1% of voters in these states swung the entire election in Trump's favor. Clinton only needed to win about 0.1% more of the vote in Michigan and 0.4% more of the vote in Wisconsin and Pennsylvania in order to prevail in the Electoral College, 278 votes to 260. That's 10,000–46,000 voters per state in states with 6 to 12 million people! In total, just 79,316 voters cost Clinton the White House.[29]

This electoral breakdown makes the causes of Trump's victory too numerous for analysis. After all, many aspects of the election could have tipped 0.1–0.5% of voters in key states towards Trump. But as we continue with our list of major causes, one commonality emerges: corruption.

Areas of Michigan, Wisconsin, Ohio, and Pennsylvania have been disproportionately affected by the decline of heavy industry, steel, and coal. They've suffered severely from the outsourcing of jobs overseas, population loss, and urban decay—a monumental case of decreasing greatness. These trends have affected many other U.S. states as well since the 1980s, but few have been harder hit than the Rust Belt. Voters experiencing decline, forsaken by the political establishment, and cynical about globalization—whom could they trust?

Even Democrats ought to recognize that the general election gave little meaningful choice to voters concerned with political and economic elites selling out ordinary Americans. The Clinton name is associated with free trade, first with Bill signing NAFTA into law and negotiating China's ascension to the WTO, and then with Hillary's support for the Trans-Pacific Partnership as secretary of state. Then, since resigning her role as secretary of state, Clinton gave a series of speeches to corporate groups engaged in lobbying the government, including some associated with the 2008–2009 crisis—and they gave her $21.7 million in fees.[30] She also received over $623 million in large donations to her campaign and brought in $598 million more in donations to her associated political committees. Furthermore, she benefitted from $204 million of super PAC spending and, apparently, support from Clinton Foundation donors.[31]

To make matters worse, Clinton's campaign made no secret of exploiting unpopular Supreme Court opinions. Seeking to capitalize on *McCutcheon*, Clinton asked her wealthiest supporters to give $300,000 or more *each* to the Hillary Victory Fund.[32] Taking advantage of *Citizens United*, pro-Clinton super PACs nearly tripled the amount raised by pro-Trump super PACs.[33] Clinton's

$1.4 billion war chest did not bode well for accountability to ordinary Americans, and voters knew it.[34]

The Democratic Party's distortion of democracy made one of Trump's most questionable features appear ethical—his use of $66 million of his own fortune to purchase a viable candidacy and outlast his rivals in the Republican primaries. Striking down the limit on self-financing by presidential candidates, *Buckley v. Valeo* posited that a large expenditure of personal wealth "reduces . . . dependence on outside contributions and . . . counteracts the coercive pressures and attendant risk of abuse."[35] This 1976 reasoning cast doubt on Clinton's campaign financing and Trump eagerly appropriated it on Twitter: "By self-funding my campaign, I am not controlled by my donors, special interests or lobbyists. I am only working for the people of the U.S.!"[36]

In any reasonable world, that argument would have fallen flat. Trump was on his way to obtaining $850 million from his supporters, and his plans to profit from his $66 million investment in the presidency were ongoing.[37] But before the primaries, soon-to-be candidates delayed entering the race in order to coordinate with super PACs. These "shadow campaigns" provided their candidates "with tens of millions of dollars in chartered planes, luxury hotel suites, opposition research, [and] high-priced lawyers."[38] Then, after they officially declared, five of the top Republican primary candidates auditioned privately for $889 million in support pledged by the Koch Brothers and 450 members of their political cabal.[39] By the time the general election rolled around, Trump's personal fortune seemed like the cleanest source of campaign funds around.

Rust Belt voters don't blame skyscrapers, beauty pageants, casinos, or *Celebrity Apprentice* for their postindustrial woes. But most of them do blame duplicitous politicians, global trade, and an elite class of donors and spenders. If Bill Clinton and Barack Obama betrayed them, could Wall Street Hillary and her super PAC army be expected to do otherwise?

"Drain the swamp!" Trump chanted. "Make America Great Again!" he promised. Wearing a baseball cap and speaking about trade and industry in combative, nationalist terms, the paradox of the people's billionaire pushing the public interest from his Manhattan penthouse morphed into something believable, the tough-talking boss who's got your back, the only figure who could stand up to Mexican outsourcing and Chinese imports. Hillary's "Overturn *Citizens United* via constitutional amendment" was utter hypocrisy, given her fundraising profile. And her "Together We're Stronger" made no sense to working-class voters forgotten by the party sworn to protect them. These slogans never landed, but Hillary's "basket of deplorables" stuck like glue. Maybe that's because the use of the word "deplorable" as a plural noun and that image of her enemies contained within a basket made for one of her most spontaneous and authentic utterances.

The irony, however, is that Trump and the Republican leadership across the country were well ahead of Hillary in identifying their own basket of deplorables; and unlike her, they succeeded in excluding them from the political process. That brings us to another form of corruption that contributed to Trump's victory.

In 2008, Obama won Michigan, Wisconsin, Pennsylvania, plus Florida, North Carolina, and Ohio. In 2012, he won them all minus North Carolina. The emergence of a viable, progressive black candidate forced modern Republicans to relearn what past defenders of white, wealthy, landowner privilege had always known. If you can't restrict the participation of minorities and the disaffected poor, Republican victories will become ever more difficult to engineer. The criminal levels of gerrymandering that maintained socioeconomic and racialized patterns of political exclusion in state legislatures and Congress have no efficacy when it comes to the presidency. And so, after Obama's 2008 victory, Republicans doubled down on the old strategy of restricting voting rights.

Seven of the eleven states with the highest African American turnout in Obama's first election passed laws that made it more difficult to vote. Nine of the twelve states with the greatest Hispanic population growth since 2010 enacted new restrictions.[40] And after Obama prevailed in 2012, the five Republican justices of the Supreme Court joined the political exclusion effort in *Shelby County v. Holder*.

Their majority opinion struck down the federal pre-clearance requirements contained in Section 5 of the Voting Rights Act.[41] Pursuant to Section 5, states with the most egregious histories of voter suppression were forced to seek the federal government's permission prior to changing their election procedures. That provision protected minorities' right to vote for nearly 50 years until Chief Justice Roberts's majority opinion announced, effectively, that racism was over.

The court correctly noted that "voter registration and turnout numbers in the covered States have risen dramatically" since the preclearance provision had gone into effect.[42] But, rather than evidence of the beneficial effects of preclearance requirements, the Republican justices considered this evidence of discriminatory effect—discrimination against states that had cleaned up their acts, a constitutional violation of their equal sovereignty by a vindictive federal government.

The same day the *Shelby County* majority opinion was published, Texas moved forward with a voter ID law that had been blocked by the preclearance section of the act just the year before. In short time, 8 of the other 15 states monitored most closely because of their histories of racist laws followed Texas's lead.[43] Overall, 18 of the 22 states that passed restrictive voting measures since 2012 did so through law-making bodies controlled by Republicans.[44]

But hindsight isn't necessary to shed critical light on the decision. In the year preceding Obama's reelection, 180 or more restrictive voting bills cropped up in 41 states. And in the year and a half prior to *Shelby County*, 13 or more laws were blocked by Section 5. Perhaps more important than blocking laws was Section 5's function of preventing discriminatory laws from being passed to begin with. Upon requests by the Department of Justice for information on potential discriminatory character of proposed laws, 262 proposed changes had been modified or abandoned across the nation in a single six-year period.[45] In sum, the justices must have realized that discrimination wasn't over and that preclearance remained a vital tool.[46]

Trump's candidacy came in the first presidential election held since *Shelby County*. African American turnout was down considerably in several key states that had recently enacted voting restrictions, including Wisconsin and Florida. Election watchers bore witness to restrictions and even abolitions of early voting, strategic voter ID laws, the purging of voting rolls, and polling places being closed, moved further away from diverse neighborhoods, or having their hours restricted.[47] These restrictions were added to a nation without a national voting holiday, without even a rule that the vote be held on a weekend—a nation of millions of voters without health insurance suffering from curable diseases and injuries, a nation chronically segregated by race and income, and often burdensome, if not impossible, to navigate through public transportation.[48]

Not only did Trump prevail, but both Houses of Congress remained in Republican hands. Given Hillary's popularity with African American and Hispanic voters, new voting rights restrictions could have been sufficient to produce Trump's victory (sustained, as it was, by such small margins in a few key states).

The predictable effect of *Shelby County* raises the possibility of a corrupt ulterior motive. Chief Justice Roberts, the author of the majority opinion, and Samuel Alito, who signed onto it, were both nominated to the court by President George W. Bush. And Bush owed his presidency to the court's 5-4 decision in *Bush v. Gore*, which stopped the Florida recount in the 2000 presidential election. While it was not as decisive of an election as *Bush v. Gore*, the holding in *Shelby County* increased the odds that Republicans would prevail in the next senate and presidential contests. That outcome was necessary to preserve the Republican majority on the court, as Trump's election and appointment of Neil Gorsuch and Brett Kavanaugh soon proved. Owing their presence on the court to this same conflict of interest, it wouldn't be surprising if Roberts and Alito failed to appreciate their own motivations.

Even though voting rights violations and massive sums of money in politics are conventional factors in American elections, they showed an unusual degree of distortion this time around. Chief Justice Roberts's assumption in *Shelby County* that racism was over clashed not only with the vital, ongoing role of the preclearance requirements, but also with voting districts drawn and redrawn to dilute minority votes, and the "New Jim Crow" of mass incarceration.[49] Plus, the decision was rendered after the

Trayvon Martin killing, a time when white civilians and police officers were apparently on a nationwide quest to murder black youth.

Either racism was increasing or the usual quantity of it was being stretched and rendered freakish by some overwhelming force. The same could be said of money in politics under the direction of the Roberts Court. *Buckley's* notions of money as speech and democracy as a market were bizarre enough, but *Citizens United's* and *McCutcheon's* approval of political responsiveness to concentrated capital was positively surreal. So were the self-financing political campaign of America's icon of conspicuous wealth and Hillary Clinton's contorted decision to capitalize on *Citizens United*, *McCutcheon*, and Wall Street patronage.

These common factors involving the electoral college, money in politics, and voting rights restrictions were surely stretched and distorted. But then a set of strange, implausible factors emerged, as though the fabric of space and time had begun to deteriorate altogether.

For the nominee of a major political party to allege that Mexican immigrants are "rapists" and propose a ban on all Muslim immigrants because "Islam hates us," was simply unheard of. But that was only the beginning, as Trump continued to substitute tweets for political discourse; bully and intimidate his opponents;[50] insult women, judges, and protesters;[51] and invigorate hate groups.[52] Trump received considerable assistance from Russia,[53] members of the media who capitalized on Gucifer's data dumps, internet trolls, and a strangely timed and recurring FBI investigation of Hillary Clinton. Exonerating Clinton but grabbing headlines in the final days prior to the general election anyhow, James Comey's investigation was easily a sufficient individual cause of Trump's narrow victory. While 57% of white voters said Trump was untrustworthy, 70 said the same of Clinton.[54]

Supreme Court sanctioned racism and plutocracy, trolls, Twitter, Vladimir Putin, Gucifer, the alt-right, Comey on the loose—it was as though the election unfolded from the canvasses of Salvador Dalí, Leonora Carrington, Yves Tanguy, and Joan Miró. But nothing really melted clocks like Trump's attacks on the independent press that had portrayed reality, reliably enough, for hundreds of years.

After a period of intense repetition and conditioning, Americans learned that information contrary to Trump's interests is fake news, organizations that criticize him or point out his lies are part of the fake news media, and Fox News, which actually does traffic in false and misleading information, is truth. (It's also the official propaganda arm of Trump's regime, just like what the Soviets and the Nazis had on their side.) Fox is joined by a decentralized network of foreign and domestic fake news entrepreneurs,[55] including those who created such real-life events as #Pizzagate. Why would someone storm a restaurant with an assault rifle in hopes of liberating children from a prostitution ring run by Hillary Clinton and John Podesta?[56] General Mike Flynn had retweeted a fake news story about Clinton and Podesta's "Sex Crimes w Children," adding the headings "U decide" and "MUST READ" on his own. In the end, just 54% of Trump's voters affirmed that #Pizzagate wasn't real.[57] Was nearly half of the Trump vote motivated by preventing the leader of a child prostitution ring from becoming president?

If sexual improprieties were one of these voters' concerns, they should have focused more on Trump. Take the case of the billionaire financier and registered sex offender Jeffrey Epstein, who was indicted for sex trafficking in 2019. His habit of soliciting erotic massages from girls as young as 14 had already come out in state and federal cases that dragged on through the 2000s.[58] In 1992, Trump held a private event at Mar-a-Lago featuring 28 "calendar girls" in which he and Epstein were the only male guests. In 2002, Trump said this about his friend: "I've known Jeff for fifteen years. Terrific guy. He's a lot of fun to be with. It is even said that he likes beautiful women as much as I do, and many of them are on the younger side."[59]

Prosecutors claim that Epstein was running a sex-trafficking scheme involving underage girls by that time. But R. Alexander Acosta, a federal prosecutor in Florida, agreed not to prosecute Epstein and to keep Epstein's victims in the dark about the arrangement. Acosta went on to become Trump's secretary of labor.[60] In 2010, Epstein refused to answer when asked in a deposition whether he and Trump had ever socialized "in the presence of females under the age of 18."[61]

This turns out to have been a very pointed question, because numerous women have gone on record accusing Trump of sexual assault. And, among them, stands a 13-year-old girl who claimed that Trump brutally raped her at one of Epstein's parties.[62] Trump was scheduled to appear in court shortly after the 2016 election, but citing death threats, the plaintiff dismissed the suit and canceled her press conference.[63] This same anonymous claimant had accused Epstein of rape as well, so perhaps some light would finally be brought to bear on this scandal in Epstein's pending trial.

But the 2019 indictment would be Epstein's last, as he was found dead in his cell in August. An independent investigation of his corpse concluded that Epstein was murdered, and a law enforcement source indicated that the cameras in his cell had stopped working, but the medical examiner ruled the death a suicide.[64] According to new federal charges, the two guards assigned to frequently monitor Epstein left him alone between 10:30 p.m. and 6:30 a.m. the night of his death. The indictment further alleges that the guards falsely signed internal documents, indicating that they checked on inmates every 30 minutes. The indictment also notes that Epstein's cellmate was transferred the day before his death.[65]

You don't have to ask what kind of conspiracy theories Trump would have launched if these events had benefited one of his opponents instead of himself. Trump and Trump Jr. rushed to implicate a former president in Epstein's death—Bill Clinton, of course.[66]

Corruption is many things, but at its root (*corruptiō* and *corrumpere* in Latin) it means "destroy" or "destruction." Beyond merely dishonest or fraudulent conduct by those in power, corruption is a process of decay and putrefaction that destroys what is pure and correct.[67] This process was already well established as regards access to political decision makers and influence over law and policy, thanks to lobbying and the donor class. It was also well underway with political speech and the formation of the popular will, thanks to unlimited political spending. But the wholesale destruction of truth and integrity hadn't quite been achieved. That's something that a reality television star and head of a branding empire was uniquely positioned to pull off. The real clincher was actually Trump's 25 years of experience with scripted wrestling events.

Trump's 2013 induction in the World Wrestling Entertainment (WWE) Hall of Fame speaks to his talent for high-impact make-believe that masquerades as reality. Heroes and villains, each with their backstories and evocative nicknames, doing battle. Trump lied repeatedly on the campaign trail, and lied or misled the public over 16,000 times in the first three years of his presidency.[68] But truth and falsehood aren't his primary concern. He's constructing a fantasy world that creates conflict, grabs headlines, and casts him as the protagonist.

WWE is the highest art in the genre. It seamlessly transitions between live and pretaped material with a live audience in tow; it ramps athletic prowess up to superhero proportions and then explodes into the emotional plane, where herculean figures experience ups and downs of soap opera proportions; and it portrays its stars on stage, around the stage, and living their lives, which are broadcast on parallel programs. Trump wove together his campaign rallies, political debates, social media messaging, internal campaign drama, and business events with similar dexterity and hyperbole, and then rammed them into the target object of the news cycle and into people's psyches through saturation and repetition.

Still, the technical term for Trump's relationship to reality isn't entertainment, fantasy, or surrealism. It's *bullshit*.

Harry Frankfurt's work *On Bullshit* explains:

> [T]he bullshitter . . . is neither on the side of the truth nor on the side of the false. His eye is not on the facts at all, as the eyes of the honest man and of the liar are, except insofar as they may be pertinent to his interest in getting away with what he says. He does not care whether the things he says describe reality correctly. He just picks them out, or makes them up, to suit his purpose.[69]

This entirely self-interested way of interacting with others suspends "the usual assumptions about the connection between what people say and what they believe."[70] Everything is part of the plot.

As WWE and Trump's rallies show, bullshit is often highly scripted; even its improvisational content tends to follow pretraced lines. Frankfurt locates its purest forms in advertising, public relations, and politics, which employ market research, public opinion polling, and psychological testing.[71] Insights gained in these places enable the bull-shitter to transcend haphazard storytelling and home in on the narratives that will resonate with the audience's needs, fears, and desires.

Ultimately, Frankfurt connects bullshit's proliferation to a breathtaking form of denial: the denial of "any reliable access to an objective reality," of "disinterested efforts to determine what is true and what is false," and even of the very "intelligibility of the notion of objective inquiry."[72] Such extreme skepticism reached a high level in the 1990s under the cynical culture of pay-to-play politics, attack ads, and shadowy outside players. But that dystopia has since been supercharged by many more layers of technology and the feverish influence of social media (android meets zombie). Amplified and inserted in just the right places, Trump's unmitigated bullshit caused society's skepticism to metastasize.

The way the Trump campaign accomplished this admits no skepticism, however. Trump's chief strategist, Steve Bannon, was vice president of Cambridge Analytica, the firm that illegally harvested data from some 50 million Facebook users. Christopher Wylie, a courageous pink-haired whistle-blower, exposed the company for using that information to create "Steve Bannon's psychological warfare mindfuck tool."[73] Those were Wylie's words for the software program that influenced voters' worldviews and choices. Such systematic manipulation of voters' perceptions of the political world amounts to the corruption—*or the destruction*—of reality.

Cosmologists and physicists provide the best explanation of these sorts of processes. Imagine speech, association, political equality, and popular sovereignty whole and intact. Then remember how they were stretched and contorted into monetary expenditures and consumer sovereignty in an economic marketplace. Imagine universal suffrage, then recall all the distortions that purged and thwarted voters. Imagine the formation of the popular will under conditions of good faith, transparency, and civility, then picture the surreal fashion in which hacking, trolling, data theft, hate, fake news, bots, and algorithms deformed the public sphere. The word for such compression and elongation by uneven gravitational forces is *spaghettification*. That's how Stephen Hawking explained what would happen to an astronaut approaching a black hole.

Because a black hole's gravitational pull increases the closer one gets to its center, our unfortunate space traveler would be stretched vertically from her head or feet—whichever end went first. And then she'd be torn apart, thanks to the fact that the unidimensional point inside a black hole has infinite mass and density, and therefore more gravitational force than any physical object can withstand. That's why one must be careful not to approach such regions of space-time, including the one described by the April Revelations.

I understand that there's another story to be told, one about human choice, not human susceptibility to outside forces. When the Supreme Court turned money into speech, corporations into citizens, and democracy into a marketplace, everyone could have refused to play along—candidates, parties, and interest groups included. Of course they would have risked losing ground to their counterparts who trafficked in influence and abused power, but integrity has never come free from sacrifice. It wouldn't be such a virtuous trait if it involved no risk and required no courage. As for Trump and his illiberal entourage, their bullshit (in the technical sense of the word) was on full display. Nobody had to buy into the reality they were selling.

But I find that story of rational choice unpersuasive in Trump's case, because the reality he sold wasn't waiting inertly on a shelf to be imbibed just by those who uncorked it. To begin with, it was manufactured through lies, hoaxes, hacks, and the theft of people's social media profiles, and, to continue, it took over the news cycle and people's social media feeds without popular consent. The same goes for the generations of Americans born into that underlying regime of government by and for the wealthy—they didn't consent to that bullshit (in the popular sense of the word).

In sum, Americans made a choice at the voting booth, but standard principles of conscious choice didn't apply. Again, astrophysics provides the relevant parallel. Space and time curve in the vicinity of a black hole. The closer you get, the fewer the pathways that lead away. Beyond a certain point of proximity, an object can even propel itself away from a black hole at the speed of light and still be sucked in. That point is known as the event horizon, and I believe the nation reached its political equivalent just before November 2016.

POPULAR DEMAND AND
POLITICAL SUPPLY

Under the conditions of systemic corruption described above, voters' decision-making processes had a certain desperate quality to them. A brief journey through the 2016 exit polls reveals that people were motivated to vote for Trump by forces beyond their control, and many of them did so despite their best judgment.

Trump received a surprising amount of popular support—62,979,636 votes in total. Naturally, most of those votes were virtually guaranteed for any Republican nominee. Sixty-two percent of small city and rural voters opted for Trump. And he won the suburban vote as well. Clinton prevailed only in cities of 50,000 or more residents, and there by a sound margin of 59% to 34%. This is almost exactly the same margin by which Trump carried the "protestant or other Christian" vote—a solid 58% majority. He also won a majority of the Catholic votes. And he trounced Clinton among white evangelical and born-again Christians by a spread of 81% to 16%. Next came the white vote—63% of all white males voted for Trump and so did 53% of white females (in spite of Trump's high-profile misogyny). Meanwhile, Clinton took 88% of the black vote, 66% of the Latino vote, and 65% of the Asian vote. Finally, Trump claimed the usual Republican advantage among older voters, earning 53% of votes from everyone 45 years of age and above.[74] These figures speak more to the momentum of the two-party system than to Trump's gravitational pull.

A different figure, which cut across many demographics, focuses in on the voters Trump captured on his own. Only one group gave him more support than evangelical and born-again Christians, and it was a group typically aligned with progressive candidates. Of voters who said the ability of a candidate to "bring needed change" mattered most, 83% voted for Trump. Among those who felt other qualities were more important, such as "the right experience," "good judgment," and "car[ing] about people like me," Clinton won easily—90%, 66%, and 58% respectively. This suggests that the 2016 election was determined by a desire for change over and above experience, judgment, and caring.

Other figures support this theory. A full 25% of Trump voters said their candidate did not have the temperament to be president and that they had an overall unfavorable opinion of him. When Trump voters were asked how they would feel if their candidate were elected president, 17% said they would be concerned.[75] Had even a tenth of these 17–25% of Trump supporters abstained or cast their votes for a third-party candidate in key battleground states, Clinton would have won. But in spite of their conscious appreciation of the dangers, something was pulling this sizable chunk of voters towards Trump.

The prioritization of needed change above other considerations aligned with voters' socioeconomic status. Of noncollege-educated whites, Trump won 72% of the male vote and 62% of the female vote—9% higher than his support from white males and white females overall. College graduates preferred Clinton to Trump by the slightest of margins (46 to 45%), but voters who had attended graduate school solidly supported her, 58% compared to just 37% for Trump. This chasm between less educated and more educated voters suggests many things, but one of them relates to needed change. Because educational achievement is highly correlated with social and economic mobility, it could be the case that the stagnation and hopelessness of many less-educated Americans turned "needed change" into an overriding demand.

Several measurements of economic well-being support this intuition. The wealthy broke nearly evenly for each candidate; those who earn $50,000–$99,000 preferred Trump by a slim margin; and those who earn under $50,000 narrowly voted for Clinton.[76] That final margin should have been stronger for a Democratic candidate, but the dynamic aspect of economic well-being proved even more disastrous for Clinton. When voters were divided along the lines of whether their families' financial situation was better or worse in the present compared with a year ago, a stunning finding emerged. Of those whose families were doing better compared to a year ago, 72% voted for Clinton. Of those doing worse compared to a year ago, 78% voted for Trump. Perceived or actual economic decline worked decisively in Trump's favor.

Needed change related to economic decline, whether real or merely perceived.

The same held true for another dynamic measurement: voters' predictions about whether life for the next generation of Americans would be better or worse. Of those who believed they would have similar or better lives, less than 40% voted for Trump. But of those who believed that life for the next generation of Americans would be worse, 63% voted for Trump.[77] Predictions of future decline fed the demand for needed change almost as much as current decline did.

Whose experiences of decline mattered most? Trump lost the Latino, Asian American, and African American votes by large margins. He also lost the urban and nonreligious vote. Hence, we're speaking more about white, religious, rural Americans' sense of well-being. By voting for Trump, these groups hoped to defend and improve their position in society. And that position was more precarious than usual. In terms of actual decline, at least 46 million Americans were living in poverty by 2010, the worst level ever recorded by the Census Bureau in the 52 years it had been keeping track. As for perceptions of future decline, another key point was reached in 2010: beyond those first 46 million people, another 51 million Americans were near poverty, meaning that about one in three Americans were poor or in serious risk of becoming poor.[78]

Trump captured the "needed change" and "economic decline" vote for three sets of reasons.

First, Trump appealed to the conscious, rational minds of those who needed change. First, he promised to bring back jobs, improve infrastructure, and generally start winning again. Second, he constantly portrayed Hillary as *criminally* untrustworthy and as part of the elite. That was Trump's rational pitch.

Second, Trump appealed to white voters' psychological needs. The first is ego justification, "the need to develop and maintain a favorable self-image and to feel valid, justified, and legitimate as an individual actor." The second is group justification, "the desire to develop and maintain favorable images of one's own group and to defend and justify the actions of fellow ingroup members."[79] These needs relate to self-esteem, identity, and community. They're present at all times, but they cry out in times of economic and social decline. Trump absolved white voters of responsibility for personal and national decline by finding others to blame.

Furthermore, Trump reinforced fears that Americans were under threat from these others. His "law and order" platform and thinly veiled racism served the same purpose. Because no Republican was going to get the black vote anyhow, why not appeal to racists? Of the 50% of white voters who said blacks were treated fairly by police (in the midst of all those officer-involved deaths), eight in ten voted for Trump.[80]

Trump's campaign had learned from the global rise of illiberal populism. Seen across much of Europe, a common electoral offer was outperforming expectations. It consisted not only in a justified dose of anti-elitism, faith in ordinary people, localism, and condemnation of corruption, but also in a worrisome combination of xenophobia, racism, sexism, strongman-style leadership, and disdain for the rule of law and independent media. Rising economic insecurity, including competition between citizens and immigrants, and declining political efficacy were exacerbating ethnic and cultural tensions across much of the democratic world. Independently of that, all democracies have their "silent majority," the group of citizens, though not necessarily a numerical majority, who have been uncomfortable with cosmopolitanism and gains for women, homosexuals, transgender persons, other minorities, and immigrants all along.[81] The insight that Trump would have immediately sniffed out (even if Bannon hadn't rubbed his nose in it) is that economic insecurity can be harnessed to produce a cultural backlash against the outgroups that could be blamed for that rising sense of decline—a backlash against everyone who's not native, white, Christian, patriotic, and otherwise culturally pure.

Economic insecurity and cultural backlash graph perfectly onto the conditions of the United States in 2016, but they don't explain why voters would choose a money-grubbing billionaire to respond to economic insecurity or why they'd choose a globetrotting, caviar-eating, country-club-owning New Yorker married to a foreigner to resuscitate some foundational American identity. But the paradox was especially acute on the economic insecurity front—if you're worried about current and future economic decline in the new Gilded Age, why elect a robber baron?

This brings us to the third set of reasons why Trump appealed to voters motivated by needed change and economic decline. A large body of experimental research has proven the existence of another core psychological drive, in addition to ego and group justification. According to experiments in numerous countries and cultures, people are "motivated to defend, bolster, and rationalize the *social systems* that affect them—to see the status quo as good, fair, legitimate, and desirable."[82]

System justification makes sense for a societal animal, one grounded not just in ego and group, but in economies, governments, and religions with complex ideological foundations. Religion, unions, and community groups have declined in America, while the economy and privatization have surged, satisfying an ever-greater part of our material and ideological needs. Trump's holdings embody the most extreme and symbolic aspects of the entire process: skyscrapers and casinos dominating the landscape, luxury resorts embodying worldly salvation, celebrity culture expressing notoriety, brands structuring and directing consumerism, pageants commodifying beauty, and reality television piercing and commercializing any authentic sense of self. Trump's properties are the mecca for *Homo economicus*, Trump's books are its commandments and prophecies, and Trump's lifestyle is its saintly example.

Those who consciously celebrate American capitalism tend to focus on the likes of Bill Gates, Steve Jobs, Warren Buffett, Elon Musk, Henry Ford, John Galt, and Howard Roark. But Trump never makes that list, at least not in the minds of the business nobility. Amidst the creators and the inventors, the libertarians, and the free market theorists, Trump stands in disrepute—something to do with that foul-smelling combination of inherited wealth, multiple bankruptcies, an ego-driven brand, political cronyism, and frequent legal and ethical controversies. But the unconscious mind isn't dissuaded by such factors. That's the first truly surprising thing about system justification. Our powerful need to rationalize and support dominant social systems flies beneath the radar of conscious awareness.

When it comes to the subconscious drive to justify American plutocracy and crony capitalism, the question is, who really embodies profit, materialism, and greed? That's the Donald, the public figure best known for stripping American capitalism naked and fondling it in front of the masses. That's who people obsessed with wealth and success dream about. Psychologist Kelly Bulkeley of the Sleep and Dreams Database confirms that Trump "appears in dreams the way a king or high priest might have functioned in other civilizations." As professor of neurology Patrick McNamara puts it, Trump "wants to be in your consciousness."[83]

Everyone expects unequal social systems to be justified by the winners, whose self-esteem, identity, family, and survival interests are tied to the perpetuation of the status quo. But system justification isn't rational or self-serving at its core. After a decade of research, psychologists came to define it as the "process by which existing social arrangements are legitimized, *even at the expense of personal and group interest*."[84] It's about the hive mind, about being able to believe in the social systems that contain us, desiring to take part in whatever capacity, achieve shared reality with others, and feel safe and secure on an even deeper level than economic well-being. That's why people accept and support the social system "even if that system entails substantial costs and relative few benefits for them individually and for the community as a whole."[85] Ego and group justification be damned. An overriding factor summons the mind.

But, no matter how subconscious the motive, surely there's a limit to what people are willing to justify. At the extreme coordinates announced by *McCutcheon*, Gilens, Page, and Piketty, would system justification really still operate to Trump's benefit?

This is where the fourth of the April Revelations comes in: Psychologists found in 2014 that *greater* powerlessness tends to lead to *greater* popular justification, not rejection and revolution.[86]

Although this effect is counterintuitive, its cause isn't. Economic and political powerlessness is disconcerting, scary, and alienating. As powerlessness increases, so do the psychological needs to "reduce uncertainty, manage threat, and uphold a sense of socially shared reality."[87]

Those are precisely the needs that people satisfy by justifying the social systems upon which society is based.

If this finding is correct, then voters most concerned
with needed change and economic decline would have
been drawn to Trump even more strongly than other
kinds of voters. Besides his material and psychological
appeals as a populist, Trump's conspicuous wealth and
unabashed self-interest would have exerted their own
gravitational pull. Victims of systemic corruption would
be subconsciously attracted to someone so uniquely
poised to employ political power corruptly. They could
be expected, as the researchers put it, to "serve as accom-
plices . . . in their own subjugation."[88]

Now that's *Homo economicus*! The notion of a new species of human isn't just a clever jab at those who are most
single-minded in their pursuit of economic self-interest. I
see *Homo economicus* as referring to something much
broader—the cognitive and behavioral tendencies of
human beings socialized under neoliberal conditions.
Those conditions include rights without responsibilities,
consumerism, de-unionization, deregulation, privatization, commodification, corporate welfare, and austerity
(cuts to education, health care, housing, poverty relief,
and retirement security). This species has little choice but
to satisfy its epistemic, existential, relational, and affec-
tive needs through an emaciated social order. With capitalism and democracy out of balance and corrupted,
generations of plutocracy have ensued, bringing about a

collective psychological transformation. That's what made Trump's greed attractive instead of repugnant.

So here's the thought experiment I've been hinting at:

The American political system has been drawn beyond the event horizon and into a political black hole. Cosmologists posit that at the center of each black hole lies a unidimensional point of infinite mass and density. That "singularity" exerts such high gravitational pull that space and time curve around it and the laws of physics break down.

Whatever passes the event horizon has lost the battle and is en route to being captured—to merging, really, with the singularity. Singularities are special because of their infinite density and mass, which exert that extreme gravitational pull upon objects with any mass of their own; hence the distortion and spaghettification of those objects when they get too close. But merging with a singularity doesn't represent the end of the line. Black holes captivate cosmologists and science fiction fans because they're the only known objects in the universe that could literally tear a hole in the fabric of space-time, creating an opening to another galaxy or even another dimension.[89]

Now, what's so special about the Seven Princes of Hell from Satan to Mammon? Their infinite manifestation of a particular sin: Satan, wrath; Lucifer, pride; Asmodeus, lust; Mammon, greed . . . They're all singularities. And remember, these demons used to be angels. Their rebellion against God came as a sign that their virtue had been exhausted. As they fought, lost, and were cast down to Hell, it was as though they imploded, acquiring infinite sin in the place of their prior light. So too with black holes. They used to be stars, but when the source of their light expired, they caved in on themselves, acquiring infinite density in the place of their prior warmth and brilliance.

Like gravitational singularities, demonic singularities are also thought to act as transport mechanisms. Demons come to tempt and manipulate human beings in order to capture their souls and take them to Hell. Gravitational singularities are hidden from the view of everyone outside the event horizon, because no light can escape from within that region—a hypothesis known as "cosmic censorship." Only after being spaghettified and torn apart by that vicious gravity could one really know what lies beyond, like submitting fully and irrevocably to a demon's force.

I posit an analogous theory of Trump's victory and presidential regime. The infinite property at the center of it all is greed, to which American plutocracy and *Homo economicus* were attracted and into which they merged. Beyond capturing the nation, the Trump singularity tore a hole in the fabric of political space-time, creating an opening to a galaxy some light years away from the plutocratic one we occupied in 2016. That neighboring galaxy is called Kleptocracy and the United States had never ventured into it before.

But an early observer did see union with Mammon (and his infinite greed) as a porthole to another dimension. He called it *The Inferno*.

5 OUT FROM THE EIGHTH CIRCLE OF HELL

By the end of 2018, the U.S. federal government was holding nearly 15,000 migrant children in camps.[1] In April of that year, the Trump regime announced its zero-tolerance approach to immigration, which included the policy of separating children from their parents at the border. But in truth, the regime began separating children a full year earlier.[2] When the House of Representatives Oversight Committee forced the Trump administration to disclose the details, it learned that 2,648 children had been taken from their parents. Nine of them were less than one year old. Nine more were under the age of two. These 18 infants and toddlers were forcibly removed for periods ranging from 20 days to 6 months.[3]

Under Trump's immigration policies, it has long been clear that migrant children could be denied contact with their parents, legal representation, education, and play-time. But we recently learned that they've also been denied showers, soap, toothbrushes, blankets, beds, and adequate food.[4] Seven of them have died in custody. And Florida Congressman Ted Deutch released documents showing hundreds of allegations of sexual abuse at child detention centers.[5]

In 2019, the Trump regime went to federal court to establish the legality of its vicious cruelty. Justice Department lawyer Sarah Fabian argued that children could be deprived of sleep, blankets, toothbrushes, and soap without violating the legal requirement of "safe and sanitary" conditions at temporary detention facilities.[6] After all, things could be worse. Inspectors had found nooses hanging from the air vents in 15 of the 20 adult cells they examined during an unannounced visit.[7] Other exposés have documented adults—including the parents of the child detainees—held in such overcrowded conditions that they apparently couldn't sit or lie down for a week at a time.[8]

Fabian appeared before the U.S. Court of Appeals for the Ninth Circuit on June 18, 2019. In the weeks just prior, Trump and four of his children—Donald Jr., Eric, Ivanka, and Tiffany—enjoyed VIP accommodations at the InterContinental Hotel in London. State department contracts put the price of the Trump family's "luxurious and relaxing base . . . with royal connections in exclusive Mayfair" at $1,223,230.[9] That's the bill that taxpayers paid. Even the White House is too spartan for Trump, whose frequent stays at Mar-a-Lago are projected to cost taxpayers nearly $1 billion over two presidential terms.[10]

Naturally, some of those $1 million per day costs are paid by the government to the Trump Organization, which runs "the winter White House" at a profit. Similarly, the U.S. government has been paying rent at Trump Tower in Manhattan to accommodate Melania's security detail.[11] Not only are taxpayers on the hook for the Trump family's lavish lifestyle, but Trump makes millions by skipping his political day job to tee off at his golf courses and vacation at his posh properties.[12] He carries out his presidential duties, including matters of national security, from those properties—again, at significant cost to taxpayers. On the other hand, perhaps this aids government efficiency, as Trump has selected at least eight members of his private clubs for administration posts, including four ambassadorships.[13] But I digress.

Would you believe that this spoiled squanderer is the one denying child detainees bathing facilities, beds, blankets, soap, toothbrushes, and even sleep? True to form, Trump detains those children and their parents at considerable profit. He maintains the same policy for suffering as he does for luxuriating—either way, it's all about the money.

GOVERNMENT BY THIEVES

While the InterContinental, Mar-a-Lago, and Trump Tower represent the peak of opulence, those cells and holding pens aren't cheap either. A network of temporary detention camps holding migrant children has charged taxpayers $775 per child per night.[14] That's $100 more per night than a deluxe guest room at the Trump International Hotel in Washington, D.C.[15] Caliburn International Corp., which owns one of the companies charging just $750 per night, remarked that Trump's policies had produced "significant growth" in profits.[16] That growth has made the detention of migrant children a $1 billion dollar industry, with one player, Southwest Key Programs, obtaining $458 million in government contracts in 2018. Its chief executive, Juan Sánchez, made $1.5 million in 2016—or, in the currency of immigration hardliners, the daily cost of two thousand children's anguish.[17]

Another player, private prison firm GEO Group, provides insight into Trump's policy-making process. When Obama announced the end of private prison contracts in 2016, GEO's stock fell. The next day it gave $100,000 to a Trump super PAC; later, another $125,000; then $250,000 to Trump's presidential inauguration;[18] and finally, over $3 million to lobbying firms, including the firm owned by Brian Ballard, Trump's campaign finance chairman in Florida.[19] In February of 2017, Jeff Sessions reversed Obama's decision. Two months later, Trump gave GEO a 10-year, $110 million contract to build and run a detention center, which is chump change compared to the $440 million in revenue that GEO expects the facility to earn.[20] In total, its contracts with Immigration and Customs Enforcement amount to nearly $500 million, and its stock has risen about 60% since Trump was elected.[21]

Should we be surprised that GEO is almost entirely tax exempt?[22] That it continues to donate hundreds of thousands of dollars illegally to conservative super PACs?[23]

Or that, after receiving a 10-year contract from Trump, GEO brought its wardens and executives to the 800-acre Trump National Doral Resort for four days of dining and golfing?[24] Such things are the predictable outcomes of our new system of government.

Under a kleptocratic regime, it's predictable that migrant detention and child separation would be parts of a private industry that runs on taxpayer dollars doled out by a president who came to power through the industry's own generous assistance. And while those migrants and their children endure gruesome conditions and suffer the psychological trauma of forced separation, the wardens and prison executives eat Trump steaks and play golf at Trump's resort at taxpayers' expense. Not to mention the contrast between migrant detention conditions and the million-dollar-a-day lifestyle that Trump and his children maintain at taxpayers' expense, with some of those millions then funneled back into Trump's own properties.

While those properties aren't tax exempt like GEO Group, Trump passed tax cuts projected to save himself up to $15 million a year, Jared Kushner up to $12 million a year, Trump's heirs up to $4.5 million, and his inner circle—including Wilbur Ross, Linda McMahon, Betsy DeVos, Steven Mnuchin, and Rex Tillerson—another $4.5 million each per year.[25] In a government of thieves, this is how law and policy are supposed to work.

Though economically significant, Trump's tax cuts are probably the least repugnant example of his self-dealing. They certainly don't rival his for-profit child detention racket, but many of his other policies do show that same determination to sacrifice the innocent, the vulnerable, and the future for private gain.

Bringing in $107 million in private funding, Trump's presidential inauguration raised twice as much money as any before it. FEC filings show that "48 people or corporations gave $1 million or more," with the fossil fuels and extractive industries providing a disproportionate share of those funds.[26] Those industries now benefit from Trump's "aggressive efforts to weaken federal rules aimed at limiting pollution in streams and wetlands, cutting back on greenhouse gases and closing coal-burning power plants."[27] They also benefit from Trump's decision to scrub climate change mitigation from the policy agenda and withdraw from the Paris Agreement.

Trump first appointed Scott Pruitt, a climate change denier, to head the Environmental Protection Agency. While attorney general for the state of Oklahoma, Pruitt "acted in close concert with oil and gas companies to challenge environmental regulations, even putting his letterhead to a complaint filed by one firm, Devon Energy."[28] Immediately upon assuming control of the EPA, Pruitt acted to the benefit of Dow Chemical. Dow's chairman and CEO, Andrew Liveris, contributed $1 million to Trump's inauguration and was then tapped by Trump to lead his Manufacturing Jobs Initiative. As head of the EPA, Pruitt "reject[ed] scientists' findings that chlorpyrifos, sold by Dow and banned from homes because of its dangers to the brains of children, should be banned from use on farms."[29] Pruitt has taken similar actions regarding other toxins, while the EPA itself has come under attack by Trump, who proposed a 31% budget cut for the agency in 2018, 23% in 2019, and 31% for 2020.[30]

Next comes Gary Cohn, the former president and CEO of Goldman Sachs who was retooled as Trump's chief economic adviser and director of the National Economic Council. On the campaign trail, Trump took a stance against the financial regulations passed after the 2008–2009 crisis. In the first month after his election, Goldman's stock rose by 34%. Cohn owned roughly $210 million in Goldman stock at the time.[31] After Cohn's appointment, Goldman Sachs benefited from a rule change regarding insuring against certain high-risk trades.[32]

Trump has also leaned the way of Secretary of Education Betsy DeVos by proposing to cut $7–10 billion from education spending. DeVos' family has funded right-wing think tanks that would privatize education—including the Mackinac Center for Public Policy, the Heartland Institute, and the Acton Institute. They wish to route people's money for education into a "marketplace of freely competing private providers," thus creating a larger arena for private profit. To fuel this agenda, DeVos has even diverted Coronavirus relief funds intended for poor students to benefit wealthy private schools.[33]

As part of what Stephen Bannon called "the deconstruction of the administrative state," Congress and federal agencies under Trump derailed over 90 regulations in his first one and a half months in office.[34] These actions have benefited the usual suspects, including Wall Street banks, gun sellers, telecommunications companies, and polluters.[35]

One particularly egregious move came less than two months into his first term, when Trump signed a bill to repeal a rule under the Dodd-Frank financial reform law that required oil and mining companies to disclose their payments to foreign governments.[36] A crucial transparency and integrity measure, the rule aimed to prevent the corruption of foreign governments and to publicize the transfer of consumers' and investors' money by multinationals to foreign oligarchs. Its repeal occurred while former Exxon Mobil CEO Rex Tillerson was serving as Trump's secretary of state. Tillerson had opposed transparency measures and his (former) company is a major beneficiary of the change.

Could anything be more treacherous than selling out children, the environment, posterity, and financial stability for personal gain? Only one kind of treachery harms the political community more deeply: treason.

The Mueller Report, congressional documents, and court records have revealed some 140 contacts between Russian nationals and WikiLeaks, on the one hand, and Trump and his associates on the other.[37] While Trump's lawyer, Michael D. Cohen, was communicating with the Kremlin and Russian oligarchs about the prospects for a Trump Tower in Moscow, and while Trump made favorable statements about Russia during his campaign, the Kremlin carried out a covert operation to get Trump elected.[38] Cohen later lied to Congress about Trump's involvement and knowledge of these discussions, as well as their duration.[39]

Other people close to Trump, such as Roger Stone, also made false statements, tampered with witnesses, and obstructed the Russia inquiry.[40] Unbeknownst to voters, Trump's own conversations about the Moscow tower continued until the day he won the election.[41] These contacts were ongoing in June 2016, when Russian government hackers were finally discovered and kicked off the Democratic National Committee's computer network.[42]

Also in June of 2016, Donald Trump, Jr., senior adviser Jared Kushner, and campaign chairman Paul Manafort met with Russians at Trump Tower to obtain "dirt" on Hillary Clinton. Presumably as part of the effort to gain a foreign nation's assistance in winning the White House, Manafort and deputy campaign manager Richard Gates transferred polling data to a Russian-Ukrainian associate with ties to Russian intelligence.[43] That information presumably helped Russia make effective use of stolen emails, social media accounts, fake YouTube videos, troll farms, and disinformation campaigns.[44] Because this strategy helped Trump gain the presidency and Republicans in Congress then provided him the sort of immunity seen only in absolute monarchy, nobody should have been surprised by what came next.

Three years after the infamous Trump Tower meeting, Trump said "I think I'd take it" if a foreign government offered him information on a political opponent again.[45] Initially, that statement seemed to be the scandal: the president admits he'd undermine the integrity of the election again in 2020. But Trump wouldn't just wait around for a foreign government to come forward. He would engage in a quid-pro-quo to procure that assistance, this time around from the Ukraine.

With the help of Lev Parnas and Igor Fruman, Rudy Giuliani pressured the Ukraine to announce an anticorruption inquiry into Joe Biden and his son in the lead-up to the 2020 election.[46] After Giuliani alerted Trump that the U.S. ambassador to the Ukraine was blocking the effort, Trump ordered her removal.[47] Later in 2019, on the same day Trump spoke with President Zelensky by phone, the White House budget office withheld $250 million in U.S. aid to his country.[48] Trump used that aid and a coveted White House visit to pressure Zelensky to investigate his main political rival. Though he was impeached in December 2019 by the House for abuse of power and obstruction of justice, Trump was effectively granted immunity by a show trial in the Senate. Disciplined by Mitch McConnell, Republican senators refused to allow witnesses to be called.

Trump's reliance on the likes of Giuliani, Parnas, and Fruman to induce a foreign power to affect voters' choices in 2020 suggests a deeper pattern. Born in the former Soviet Union, Parnas and Fruman have been arrested for funneling foreign money into American political campaigns, including a $325,000 donation to America First, a pro-Trump super PAC.[49] Giuliani has continued to work for numerous foreign clients while serving as Trump's personal lawyer, including pro-Russian interests in the Ukraine.[50]

That should remind readers of Paul Manafort, Trump's 2016 campaign chairman who was sentenced to 47 months of imprisonment for fraudulently concealing income from his political consulting work in the Ukraine. He received over $17 million from a pro-Russian political party between 2012 and 2014, but only disclosed his status as a foreign agent in 2017, after chairing Trump's campaign.[51] Gates also consulted for those same foreign interests and eventually pled guilty to conspiring against the United States and lying to federal agents in the Mueller inquiry.[52] Trump's first national security adviser, Michael Flynn, also pled guilty to making false statements that impeded the Russia investigation and lying about his activities as a foreign agent during the 2016 campaign.[53]

This proverbial rabbit hole illustrates how Trump's first campaign and presidential administration have corrupted American elections and violated American sovereignty. The Foreign Agent Registration Act requires foreign agents to register and disclose their activities. It arose in response to political spending by Nazi Germany to manipulate the political debate in the United States in favor of the Third Reich. The 1966 amendments to the act prohibit contributions from foreign interests in U.S. elections. They arose in response to efforts by Philippine sugar companies and a Nicaraguan dictator to influence U.S. elections. People close to Trump have a well-established tendency to violate these laws, but is Trump himself so corrupt and disloyal?

MOTHER RUSSIA

Trump's dealings with Russian oligarchs and the Russian Mafia suggest an especially corrupt relationship. Craig Unger traces it back to 1984, when Trump sold five condos in Trump Tower to David Bogatin, later revealed to be "a leading figure in the Russian Mob." After Bogatin pled guilty to a tax plot, was sentenced, and fled the United States, the government seized his properties at Trump Tower and revealed that they were purchased to launder money.[54] It was in that same year, 1987, that the Soviet government took Trump and Ivana on an all-expenses paid trip to Moscow to begin the saga of a Trump hotel across the street from the Kremlin. Over the next three decades, Trump doubled down on shady transactions involving shell companies and, most likely, some of the $1.3 trillion of illicit wealth that flowed out of the Soviet Union when it fell in 1991.[55]

A Russian mob boss infamous for his expertise in torture casts light on Trump's background. The year after he was released from a Siberian prison by a well-placed bribe, Vyachelsav Kirillovich Ivankov traveled illegally to the United States. Between 1992 and 1995, he mounted a multibillion-dollar criminal enterprise backed and enforced by "combat brigades" of former Soviet Special Forces members imported into New York City. Tracking Ivankov, the FBI discovered his frequent visits to Trump Taj Mahal in Atlantic City during a period in which the casino was laundering considerable sums of money. The

Treasury Department's Financial Crime Enforcement Network (FinCEN) went on to expose Trump's multiple failures to observe anti-money-laundering rules between 1998 and 2014, when Trump Taj Mahal finally filed for bankruptcy. In 2015, FinCEN fined Trump's casino $10 million for what the government called "significant and longstanding anti-money laundering violations."[56] That's how Trump earned the distinction of owning the casino that received the highest fine ever from the federal government. And when the FBI finally succeeded in locating Ivankov, they found him living in a luxury condo at Trump Tower.[57]

In its 2015 press release, FinCEN marveled at how Trump failed to take action in response to its findings. The agency had warned multiple times that Trump Taj Mahal was severely vulnerable "to criminals, terrorists, and other bad actors." The casino itself had "admitted that it failed . . . to report suspicious transactions . . . to file required current transaction reports [and] to keep appropriate records."[58] But the Trump Organization still refused to take action. It's endearingly naïve that the Treasury Department couldn't wrap its mind around the fact: Trump had found his niche and would not be pressured to give up the golden goose by the mere threat of a civil penalty.

At the start of the 1990s, Trump was indebted to some 72 banks to the tune of $4 billion, $800 million of which he had personally guaranteed.[59] In his book, *The Art of the Comeback*, Trump describes his own heroism in threatening his creditors with bankruptcy proceedings that would "tie you guys up for years." Attempting to leverage his own failure, he demanded that the banks defer his loan payments and front him $65 million to weather the downturn in the real estate market.[60] Bankers declined Trump's terms and decided to recover their money by selling off Trump's properties one by one. They did grant him "an allowance" to keep his businesses running in the meantime, however, and they forgave his personal liabilities on the condition that he assist in the sales.[61]

Trump wasn't the only one defaulting on his debt. Russia defaulted on $40 billion in treasury bills in 1998. Inflation rose to over 80%, and the ruble went from 6 to the dollar to 21 to the dollar. The largest private banks failed and when the IMF bailed them out, much of that money was embezzled.[62] Where could oligarchs put their funds, besides tropical offshore accounts? The oligarchs' plight coincided with the construction of the 90-story Trump World Tower in Manhattan. Russian individuals and LLCs soon owned about a third of the most expensive units.[63]

Trump's World "Tower of Oligarchs" inspired the rebranding of six residential high-rises in southern Florida, creating "Moscow on the Beach." A 2017 report by *Reuters* found that 63 Russians invested $98.4 million in the luxury towers that bore Trump's name. But only those whose names weren't connected to Putin or the Russian mafia acted so transparently. Another 703 units were purchased using LLCs, allowing the owners to remain hidden from view.[64]

If these reports are accurate, then the Trump Organization functions as a secrecy haven for Russian wealth. As Craig Unger points out, the timing of these investments (between the late 1990s and early 2000s) allowed Trump to rise from the ashes as the host of the new show, *The Apprentice*.[65]

Trump's Russian entanglements sometimes produced embarrassing results, like the time in 2013 that police raided the Trump Tower unit directly below his own residence. Why would they do such a thing? Think Taj Mahal, but right under Trump's nose. Unit 63A of Trump Tower had become the headquarters of a money laundering operation responsible for some $100 million of former Soviet loot. Police also shut down an illegal gambling operation that occupied "the entire fifty-first floor of the building." Unger rightly notes how remarkable it is that Trump could kick off a successful presidential campaign on these very grounds, less than three years later.[66]

The evidence just keeps piling up, including the "86 all-cash purchases—a red flag of potential money laundering—of Trump properties, totaling $109 million" between 2003 to 2017 by buyers tied to Russia, and Trump's massive 2010 loan from the private-wealth division of Deutsche Bank, which was then laundering billions of dollars from Russia.[67]

Having recently travelled to Russia six times, Donald Trump Jr. admitted the obvious in 2008: "Russians make up a pretty disproportionate cross-section of a lot of our assets."[68] Was it really so surprising that Trump Jr. would go on to host that infamous meeting at Trump Tower—already a den of Russian criminals—to obtain opposition research on Hillary? Russian assistance, in the forms of hacking, trolling, and disinformation campaigns, was the most predictable thing in the world. Their American laundromat was poised to win the presidency, and Trump's adversary, no friend of Russia, was vulnerable. Trump tweeted from the campaign trail, "Russia, if you're listening, I hope you're able to find the 30,000 emails that are missing." That same day, Russia tried to hack Clinton.[69] Later, Trump admitted "the Russia thing" was on his mind when he fired James Comey.[70]

On the basis of considerable evidence, Unger concludes that Trump is a "Russian asset in the White House."[71] You might playfully say, in the language of the Emoluments Clause, that he's been given a prohibited "*Office* or *Title*" of the most infamous sort; or, more gravely, you might quote the most specific legal provision on point, 18 U.S.C. §2381, and call Trump a traitor:

> Whoever, owing allegiance to the United States, . . . adheres to their enemies, giving them aid and comfort within the United States or elsewhere, is guilty of treason and shall suffer death, or shall be imprisoned . . . and shall be incapable of holding any office under the United States.

If it weren't for the complicity of Republicans in the Senate, a full investigation would have ensued years ago. Trump enforced a policy of absolute secrecy on high-level meetings with Putin (even personally seizing the translator's notes) and then proceeded to withdraw U.S. forces from Syria, ease sanctions on a key oligarch, and float the idea of withdrawing from NATO.[72] It's clear that the obstacle to accountability isn't evidentiary in nature. But the obstacle isn't just political, either. The United States has a spiritual problem on its hands.

CAPTURE BY EVIL

Trump's nefarious schemes require that we recalibrate our sense of corruption. Justifying a constitutional prohibition on emoluments, Alexander Hamilton warned that foreign governments could "corrupt [the president's] integrity by appealing to his avarice."[73] Writing in 1788, the year before the Constitution was ratified, Hamilton only contemplated a democratically elected leader, not someone who had taken control by royal birth or military victory. That's why Hamilton couldn't have conceived of a president without any integrity to corrupt in the first place, nor predicted that such a pitiful creature would be the one to prove the Federalists' constitutional design so radically unsound. Trump is the first president in American history for whom nothing but avarice holds any appeal. Pull him out of the swamp, task him with some disinterested matter of the public good, and you'd see his gills strain, his mouth contort into repetitive "O" shapes, and his suit-encrusted body thrash around the Oval Office, rage-like.

Today's political crisis pits the public and the constitutional design against a paradigm breaker, a figure who openly derides ethical principles and legal restraints. If it were only possible to appeal to the integrity of the Senate or the Supreme Court, then there'd be no extraordinary calling to answer. But Republican complicity being what it is, the American people have to look beyond the Constitution's provisions on emoluments and impeachment, and beyond the fallen institutions that are supposed to give those provisions life. Because the Constitution can be amended, it should be conceived of as an evolving foundation molded by environmental factors, experience, and, ultimately choice. But, just like a physical body, the Constitution can't animate itself. Beneath it, there's a life force. That's the level at which the crisis strikes.

From what source can the people possibly draw strength?

Assuredly, this presidency amounts to a dark night of the soul, extended near eternal by the unfolding of so many disturbing revelations. Assuredly, this political abyss of 2016–2020 has subjected all lovers of democracy to betrayal, hopelessness, and suffering. Our existential crisis reminds me of a great Italian poet who faced at least as much cruelty and corruption as we have, but still progressed.

At the start of his fourteenth-century poem *The Inferno*, Dante Alighieri finds himself in a dark wood. He cannot say just how he entered, only that he was too sleepy to notice that he "had gone astray from the one true path."

Coming to his senses, he realizes he's ventured to the lowest part of a valley that pierces his heart with fear. But he gazes upwards to find "the warm rays of the planet that gives light to guide our steps." His fear subsides, and his heart finally calms after enduring that "long and piteous night."

Looking back at the place he had been poised to enter, his mind beholds "the passage that had never let anyone escape alive before."[74] He begins climbing back up the hillside, but his way is blocked by a leopard, then a lion, and finally a she-wolf. This is Dante's acknowledgment that his will and intellect have been overcome by lust, pride, and avarice (or fraud). His hopes fade as he's numbed by fear. Lost in weakness and dread, he retraces his steps back down "where the sun is mute."[75]

Are you not reminded of the nation's plight under Trump? And of Mammon's singularity, which consumes all light?

Dante begins his journey into Hell through that deathly passage and at Hell's gate encounters the oft-quoted words, "Abandon all hope, ye who enter here."[76] Also inscribed on that portal are other words much-ignored by popular understandings of Hell: "Justice moved my great maker in my design, I was created by the primal love, wisdom supreme and potency divine,"[77] a sign (literally) that even the worst realm of agony is part of a larger, more benevolent plan.

Dante's carves out a special place in Hell for corruption:

> Because only human beings can commit a fraud, this is the sin God most resents . . . and a man may use fraud on one who trusts him or one who invests no special confidence. In the latter way he breaks the natural bond of love that exists among all humanity, and thus is sent to . . . the nests of hypocrites, flatterers, thieves . . . simoniacs and cheats, swindlers and pimps and all such excrement.[78]

But fraud in violation of trust is still worse, because it violates a special bond. Think of the trust deposited in an American president and the special bond that's supposed to exist between him and the people. Dante notes that this type of fraud lands a soul in the very center of Hell.

Dante's *Inferno* is organized into nine circles, each progressively worse than the one before it. While mere greed lands souls in the fourth circle, guarded by Pluto, the Greek god of wealth, corruption takes souls twice as far, to the eighth. The eighth circle's many "evil ditches" are populated by different groups of sinners, organized according to the type of corruption they perpetrated. In the third ditch, Dante finds those who trafficked in holy things, such as ecclesiastical offices (the simoniacs).

In the fifth ditch, he finds the barrators who bought and sold public offices and the grafters who corrupted politics by "changing *no* to *yes* for plunder."[79] Corrupt politicians are immersed in cauldrons of boiling pitch. When the pain is too much, and they surface, demons shred their bodies with their claws and grappling hooks. All that flaying forces the sinners to remain where their own meat is cooked through by "gluey coating," which symbolizes their sticky deals.[80]

The eighth circle features apt descriptions of Trump and his team, including those who exploit others' passions and corrupt language to enlist people's fears in some fraudulent purpose; those who manufacture disagreements, civil strife, and political polarization; and those who falsify words and money (today's money launderers).

In the ninth circle, Dante beholds the traitors—traitors to kin, to country, guests, and benefactors. Finally, in the very center of Hell, Dante finds a three-mouthed version of Satan holding the three worst traitors in his teeth, "bloody slobber dripping down his three chins."[81] Satan's front mouth grips Judas Iscariot by the head, while the rest of him is flayed, and Satan's side mouths clench the bodies of Brutus and Cassius. Treason against God and treason against the government of man—for these acts, the greatest pain.

What's to be gained by recounting Dante's vision? To begin with, a powerful understanding of what we're facing and a plan for action. And ultimately, a happy reunion of sorts.

Dante brings us back to the Biblical frame for life after the Fall, once human beings could know good and evil and had to choose how to live. That frame juxtaposes virtue with sin, God with Satan, and ultimately salvation with damnation. Salvation and damnation both describe transformational processes of people's innermost beings, followed by a proportionate gravitational pull. God, the embodiment of infinite virtue, pulls the virtuous up to Heaven, while Satan, the embodiment of infinite sin, pulls the sinful down to Hell. Those metaphysical processes occur after death, but they are determined before it, by how people live their lives. Thoughts and deeds leave their imprint on the eternal soul, and Dante makes that point more poignantly than anyone when it comes to corrupt intentions and actions.

Most people in advanced democracies no longer take such religious descriptions seriously, but the end of faith came a moment too soon, right as religion and science were beginning to meet. Consider that sins are mostly framed as emotions. Hatred, envy, lust, pride, wrath, and greed, for example, refer first and foremost to what people feel—in the case of greed, that "excessive desire to acquire more possessions than what one needs or deserves, especially with respect to material wealth."[82] Excessive desire is an emotion, and its effects on attention, perception, and reasoning are known to produce selfish actions. Beyond their obvious influence on cognition and behavior, emotions influence our chemical and biological makeup. Their effects on cortisol and adrenaline levels, blood pressure, the chemicals we emit through our mouths (the volatolome), and even on chromosomes and mitochondrial DNA are now pushing the frontiers of chemistry and epidemiology.[83]

Once these emerging insights are combined with the psychological evidence that most people subconsciously justify the social systems that oppress them, it's no longer tenable to treat corruption as something that's "out there," separate from us. Rather, it's something in here, that takes over and transforms us.

That's something that people in our political tradition used to understand. Searching the legal canon for the underlying meaning of corruption, Laura Underkuffler transcends the categories of bribery, extortion, embezzlement, and trading in influence, and their associated elements. She also goes beyond the generally applicable "abuse of entrusted power for private gain," which fails to capture the religious and emotional dimensions that resonated with Dante and Milton. In the end, Underkuffler realizes that corruption means "the capture by evil of one's soul."[84] If soul is too strong for your taste, then feel free to substitute emotions, cognition, behavior, biochemistry, and subconscious mind in its place.

Though this might sound like a purely individual definition of corruption, Underkuffler guards against that interpretation: Corruption "is not simply an act, or a series of acts. It is the capture of individuals (*and political systems*) by corrosive, distorting, and decomposing forces."[85] "The corrupt politician," Underkuffler continues, "does not simply threaten particular individuals[—] his existence threatens the entire governmental system of reliance, trust, and the rule of law of which he is a part."[86] In this way, evil—that "fundamental disorder of the self"—soon becomes a fundamental disorder of society. The individual sins that Underkuffler uses to define evil, including greed, disloyalty, squandering, envy, and self-indulgence, then come to infest the social fabric.[87] The connection between individual and systemic corruption is also conveyed by Dante's model, in that the various iterations of corruption committed by all those souls in all those ditches represent a society that's rotten on every level.

Such understandings of corruption convey the significance of Trump's kleptocracy, which is akin to Dante's passage into Hell and to capture by Mammon and his singularity of infinite greed. They point to the moral and spiritual dimensions of the transformation bound up with systemic corruption. That process has legal and sociological dimensions as well, which the literature on comparative politics helps reveal.

As Andrew Wedeman puts it, "Kleptocracy denotes a state ruled by thieves in which corrupt officials *transform* the state into an instrument of private plunder."[88] Trump may not behave exactly like Mobutu in Zaire or Margai, Momoh, or Conteh in Sierra Leone, but overt plunder isn't the only form of kleptocracy. Wedeman also defines it as "a pervasive effort to transform the state and the economy into personal prebends for the ruler, his family, and his inner circle of cronies."[89]

Conforming to this design, Trump has placed his children and son-in-law in key positions of influence within the White House. Jared Kushner has become senior adviser and international envoy, and Ivanka Trump has become assistant to the president.[90] The 1967 anti-nepotism statute cannot keep up, having been construed by Kushner, his lawyers, and two judges on the U.S. Court of Appeals for the District of Columbia Circuit as inapplicable to White House staff jobs.[91] Just hours after Trump's inauguration, the U.S. Department of Justice issued a memorandum opinion, finding that U.S. law "exempts positions in the White House Office from the prohibition on nepotism in 5 U.S.C. § 3110."[92]

The opportunities for bribery, extortion, and trading in influence could hardly be more plentiful. Kushner's real estate business received $90 million in foreign funding from an "opaque offshore vehicle" in 2017 alone.[93] He has worked with state-owned enterprises in China and currently works with some of China's top leaders.[94] I should add that Kushner's insensitivity to anticorruption law is predictable, given that he gained admission to Harvard University after his father, a convicted tax evader and campaign finance law violator, donated $2.5 million to the institution.[95]

In May of 2018, the Chinese government gave Ivanka 13 trademarks, plus provisional approval for another 8, to market her products in China.[96] Just days after five of these were approved, Trump (who holds over 100 Chinese trademarks) reversed his policy on a Chinese telecommunications firm that came under fire for violating U.S. sanctions on Iran and North Korea.[97]

Like Wedeman, Sarah Chayes emphasizes the importance of personal relationships to kleptocratic regimes. Her work has unearthed the centrality of horizontally integrated networks that rub out the distinction between the public and private sector. Living in Afghanistan, Chayes noted that the president's brother owned part of the largest private bank and the largest cement factory. In Azerbaijan, she pondered how the "ruling Aliyev family owns no fewer than 11 banks and consortiums that straddle energy, real estate, infrastructure contracting and tourism." As if the similarities to the Trump family and the cabinet weren't evident enough, Chayes observed that "family members serve as ligaments binding the intertwined systems together"—a common trend among kleptocracies.[98] Integrated networks composed of Trump's family, advisers, cabinet members, and foreign allies work with "devilish creativity" to align government agencies and institutions with members' economic interests. When government departments can't be coopted, kleptocrats "disable or cannibalize them."[99]

Chayes also puts the Trump family's long history with Russian mafia and oligarchs into perspective, and possibly Trump's high-level meetings with Saudi Arabia, China, and North Korea as well. Kleptocratic networks are transnational just "like the globalized business conglomerates or drug cartels."[100] Chrystia Freeland's work on plutocrats also exposes that feature. Today's plutocrats are different from yesterday's insofar as they comprise a "transglobal community of peers who have more in common with one another than with their countrymen back home." The global superrich are "increasingly a nation unto themselves."[101] Tracking the national and international pull of Chinese and Russian oligarchs, Freeland notes that their wealth and entanglement with governments practically dictate power relations globally.[102] This shocking view of the world—the world as it is—puts Trump's involvement with Russia into context.

Chayes' formula for kleptocracy also casts the spotlight on Trump's interest in the presidential power to pardon people for offenses against the United States.[103] Kleptocratic networks "are held together by a bargain[:] Subordinate members funnel a part of their take upward to their seniors . . . In return, those at the top guarantee impunity down the line."[104]

Article 2, section 2, of the U.S. Constitution is unforgivably broad on its face: "The President . . . shall have Power to grant Reprieves and Pardons for Offenses against the United States, except in Cases of Impeachment."[105] But during the Mueller inquiry, Trump interpreted it more broadly still. "I have the absolute right to PARDON myself,"[106] he tweeted.

As you might expect, Trump's position conflicts with the one taken by the Department of Justice the day Nixon's role in Watergate became clear.[107] But under Attorney General William Barr, today's Justice Department has openly abandoned the rule of law. After public criticism by the president, it moved to reduce Roger Stone's sentence (for witness tampering and obstructing the Russia inquiry) and to dismiss Michael Flynn's conviction (after he pled guilty to making false statements during the Russia inquiry).[108]

This politicization of justice is carried out through the installation of Trump loyalists as U.S. attorneys and federal judges—the actors responsible for the fate of subordinate members of the kleptocracy. Two months after assuming office, Trump fired nearly half of the 93 U.S. attorneys and began nominating candidates for the federal bench "at a breakneck pace."[109] By November of 2019, Trump had appointed 2 Supreme Court justices, 44 Circuit Court judges, and 112 District Court judges.

According to a White House briefing, this "historic transformation of the judiciary" has "tipped the balance of numerous Federal courts to a Republican appointed majority" in order to counter the "left-wing's . . . radical agenda." Noting the surprisingly young age of many appointees, the briefing concludes that Trump's judges "are expected to give the Nation more than 2,600 years of combined judicial service."[110] Naturally, the briefing doesn't mention the recent role of independent judges in unseating corrupt regimes in Brazil, Guatemala, and South Korea.

In light of the complexity and grip of kleptocratic forms of government, Chayes draws a lesson for Americans: "These networks are like weeds, and it takes far more than the punishment of a few crimes, even spectacular ones, or the removal of a few people to fully uproot their tendrils from the economic and political institutions we hold dear."[111] Trump and his network have been digging in for years now—their roots, vines, and branches interlacing with federal institutions, laws, and policies, and connecting up with other networks at local, state, foreign, and international levels.

How should we conceive of this creeping, twisting transformation in law and society? Is there any beneficial way to experience the transplantation of Hell's eighth circle upon the United States?

When Dante strayed from the one true path, he found himself on "tangled ground . . . overlaid with harsh and savage growth, so wild and raw the thought of it still makes [him] feel afraid."[112] That reflection on the first page of his poem is followed by a noble statement of purpose: "Death scarce could be more bitter. But to draw the lessons of the good that came my way, I will describe the other things I saw."[113] Dante travelled straight into Hell and let its every detail enter his eyes, absorbing the lessons of his dark night. And at the end, he climbed back, over Satan, "into the world of light." Nearing the surface, Dante saw through a hole "those heavenly things that beautify the night." "Stars" is the last word of all three parts of Dante's *Divine Comedy*, a trilogy of light. Dante was writing the journey of his soul and, as if to prove it, he died the same year he finished *Paradiso*.

There's no denying the horror of our national journey under Trump. The only sorts of questions that remain are, What will we make of it? What kind of story are we writing in our capacity as citizens? Thus far, it's a political tragedy. We remain on the tangled ground of Trump's kleptocracy, a transnational government of flatterers, hypocrites, barrators, grafters, falsifiers, and traitors. But Dante goes through

Hell and reemerges into the world of light, resolved to follow a virtuous path.

So I ask, What was Dante's secret to getting through *The Inferno*?

CHOOSING REVOLUTION

When the beasts of pride, lust, and avarice force Dante back into the depth where the sun is mute, he makes someone out in spite of the darkness: "A shape was offered to my vision, wan as if from a long silence it had kept." When the being tells Dante that in life he was a poet under Augustus in Rome, Dante recognizes him as Virgil, "that fountainhead that spills such a mighty stream of eloquence . . . Light and glory of all poets." Already Dante's prose tells of a powerful, original source reappearing in his hour of need. His reference to light, glory, and the fountainhead are all allusions to God, but Virgil isn't God. He's a highly personalized guide back to the light. Dante proclaims his "intense love and long study" of Virgil's poetry, from which his own style is derived. It's no wonder, then, that Dante surrenders to Virgil, "my master, my authority," resting in him all hope for deliverance.[114]

In the United States, we too have a fountainhead that we've long loved and studied. It has given our country its noble style, and I believe it contains the key to our deliverance today. Here's how the Declaration of Independence described King George III's reign over the American colonies: "The history of the present King of Great Britain is a history of repeated injuries and usurpations, all having in direct object the establishment of an absolute Tyranny over these States."

The revolutionaries had their laundry list of King George's bad deeds, just as most Americans today have one for Trump. The Declaration goes on for several pages, after all. But the revolutionaries focused on the severity of those actions ("injuries" to the people's sacred rights and honor, and "usurpations," a theft of political power from its rightful source). Next, they focused on the purpose and system of government behind those injuries and usurpations—not monarchy, but *tyranny*. That word allowed years of injustice to be summoned to heart and mind with a single utterance.

Tyranny was a hard-earned collective understanding, a verdict on the status quo that resonated with the people. As the colonists awoke from centuries of custom and saw the monarchical regime for what it was, an emotional boiling point followed. The revolutionaries channeled this raw sentiment into a principled alternative to hierarchy, control, and obedience. The people should be free and equal authors of their destiny—not hog-tied subjects of an aristocracy. Relying "on the protection of divine Providence," our political forefathers pledged their "lives, fortunes, and sacred Honor" to freeing the colonies. Undertaken in the very last line of the Declaration, their commitment emanated from a transformation within the people and the national design: self-doubt had been converted into self-confidence, and hysteria into love for democracy.

The Declaration's allegation of tyranny and proposal for self-rule would lead the people to discover their potential through revolution. And it worked. The revolutionaries defeated the most powerful government in the world and established a new form of government deemed impossible by many centuries of conventional wisdom.

Which ought to remind us, the challenge isn't just to remove Trump. It's to defeat the form of government bound up with his regime and to realize our national potential for something greater. This purpose, like the establishment of democracy itself, requires an eighteenth-century understanding of political oppression. Tyranny is "the exercise of power beyond right[,] not for the good of those who are under it, but for [one's] own private, separate advantage." John Locke, who gave us this definition, advised future generations to remain vigilant because tyranny can take hold in other kinds of government besides monarchy: "[W]herever the power is put in any hands for the government of the people, and . . . is . . . made use of to impoverish, harass or subdue them . . . There it presently becomes Tyranny."[115]

Trump and his Republican loyalists assume that Americans won't awaken to the reality of political oppression. They believe we'll continue to be run ragged, divided, and distracted by Trump's outrageous regime (*harassed* or *subdued*). Meanwhile, they'll continue to reconfigure law, policy, and government institutions for private gain (*impoverished*).

The Declaration urges us to connect the dots between Trump's many intolerable acts: repeated injuries and usurpations all aimed at the establishment of an absolute tyranny. The trouble is, most Americans today have lived their entire lives (or adult lives at least) under a vaguely oppressive regime. From the 1970s to 2016, laws, policies, and institutions were unduly influenced, if not controlled, by a symbiotic relationship between public officials and business interests. What Americans think of as democracy has been plutocracy all the while.

Then along came Trump with a big idea. Why not cut out those inefficient middle-men known as politicians and bureaucrats? Why not allow the wealthy to govern directly? Convinced that this alternative promised greater profits, power, and glory, Trump became the founding father of American kleptocracy.

Had his wholesale perversion of government arisen suddenly, like a tsunami in a placid ocean of integrity, a revolutionary backlash would have been predictable. But as things stand, the prospects for such an awakening depend on a deeper realization.

Although the Declaration didn't anticipate the tyranny of greed, its author did. Over 200 years ago, Thomas Jefferson warned that the country was "headed toward a single and splendid government of an aristocracy founded on banking institutions and moneyed incorporations."

He stated that the result would be "the end of freedom of democracy" and that "the few will be ruling and riding over the plundered ploughman and beggar." The man who had provided so eloquent a basis for the Revolutionary War then suggested that the revolution must continue. His solution to government of, by, and for the wealthy was the same as his solution to monarchy: Jefferson advocated that we "crush in its birth the aristocracy of our monied corporations."[116]

In 1912, Theodore Roosevelt made a similar claim. "Behind the ostensible government sits enthroned an invisible government owing no allegiance and acknowledging no responsibility to the people," he wrote. His Progressive Party considered "the first task of the statesmanship of the day" to be the destruction of that "unholy alliance between corrupt business and corrupt politics."[117]

In 1936, Franklin D. Roosevelt voiced the same awareness by comparing systemic corruption to the tyranny at issue in 1776. He framed his progressive platform in opposition to "economic *royalists*" and "new *dynasties*" whose "*kingdoms* were built upon concentration of control over material things."[118]

The tyranny of greed has threatened self-governance since the beginning of our imperfect union. Trump's kleptocracy and the preceding 40 years of plutocracy stand as a humbling reminder of the nation's most enduring failure. These are the only political systems most of us have known, and yet our lifetimes aren't over. There is another way, the one expressed by that revolutionary intolerance of tyrants and their tyrannies, the one that unfolds from an unwavering commitment to freedom, equality, and self-governance for all. That's the spirit I offer to our vision today, the national fountainhead, which remains willing to guide us whenever we embrace it as our source and authority. But that would require a change in perspective.

There's no end to history. We're in the thick of it every bit as much as the colonists during monarchy and the working class during the Gilded Age—and we too have a vital role to play. Repeated injuries and usurpations? A despotic form of government that harasses, subdues, and impoverishes the people? If that sounds too dramatic or historical to apply to America today, then we've been socialized into the belief that self-interest and profit should be the motors of government. And that's the uncritical state of slumber that Trump has been banking on all along.

I'm going to be greedy for the United States!

The President can't have a conflict of interest!

I won't release my tax returns!

For my cabinet, I want people who made a fortune!

The prohibition on nepotism doesn't apply to the White House!

Unanimous decision in my favor on the ridiculous Emoluments Case!

Impeachment witch hunt and total exoneration!

I have the power to pardon myself!

Trump is so confident about our estrangement from the American revolutionary tradition that he has barely disguised his designs. Upon reflection, he might not even know about that tradition, which wouldn't entirely be his fault. If adequate controls against corruption had been in place, Trump would never have made it so far. Which is why this book began with a parable.

What is Donald J. Trump? Ultimately, he's a mirror of the nation's innermost pathology and dysfunction, which could no longer be tamed, papered over, or dressed up for polite company. Our demon broke free and took over. Laws and policies had fed it and it had grown strong. We had tolerated or worshipped it, and it had grown strong. But now that it's out in the open, we can finally confront it. To bring about that reckoning, we have to answer the question in an empowered fashion.

What is Trump? We get to decide in the end. We get to decide whether he succeeds in corrupting the United States and getting away with it. Trump's gravitational power is awesome indeed, but seriously, *Are we going to let this tacky, loudmouthed king of branding and luxury real estate determine the fate of the world's oldest democracy? Will we allow the country that defeated the British monarchy, slavery, Nazis, fascists, and communists to be eviscerated by this narcissistic caricature of a businessman?*

Having reframed the question, here's how my answer begins. Trump is the stress test that finally proved American democracy structurally unsound. His election and presidency have demonstrated that anticorruption law is optional in the United States. On some points it's absent, on others it's incomplete, and in most cases it's dependent on politically minded actors for enforcement. Democracy remains unfinished; and that's the evolutionary role of tyranny: to expose vulnerability and incompleteness in a political form.

All tyrannies involve the capture of state power by some outside force. King George III was a hereditary monarch. Political power accrued automatically to people in that family line and to whoever held the titles it bestowed. Monarchies can also be formed by conquest—the union of military force with political power. Whether through family lineage or military might, monarchy is tyrannical in allowing these kinds of power to dominate politics and the state. Theocracy commits the same sin by allowing religious leaders to dominate the state. Essentially, tyrannies are unholy unions between different power centers— family lineage and state, religion and state, military and state, and now business and state.

The solution comes in the form of separation. Beyond separating the country from Britain and instituting elections, the framers of the Constitution separated the powers of governance to prevent something like monarchy from arising; they separated church and state to prevent theocracy; and they instituted civilian control of the military.

If we should not be ruled by a foreign power, royal birth, religious hierarchy, or military might, why should we be ruled by wealth? Why should popular participation, elections, and law-making bow to financial power?

The status quo is surely unjust, but tyrannies aren't known for yielding to logic alone. It's up to the people to unite under a common understanding. It's up to the people to demand a separation of business and state from candidates, officeholders, and political parties.

That separation would be created by a legal architecture, which would look something like this: stricter campaign finance limits (including limits on candidate self-financing, campaign expenditures, and outside spending, plus a repudiation of Supreme Court caselaw); equitable public financing for parties and campaigns; elimination of super PACs and dark money groups; revised conflict of interest rules binding on the president, vice president, cabinet members, and members of Congress (including mandatory annual disclosure of tax returns and divestment from business holdings); enhanced rules against nepotism and trading in influence (including stricter regulations on lobbying); a comprehensive ban on gifts and benefits to supplement the Emoluments Clauses of the Constitution; new regulations on social media companies and online campaigning to account for matters of transparency, data privacy, foreign interference, and deceptive content; and new independent federal agencies to monitor and enforce such provisions.

Given the Supreme Court's ideological commitment to plutocracy, ordinary legislation wouldn't suffice. The people would have to agitate for a constitutional amendment. But other crises in U.S. history required wars (revolutionary and civil), a Constitution drafted from scratch, and many amendments. Perhaps Americans have more civic spirit and mass protests left in them. Moved by that revolutionary promise of freedom, equality, and self-government for all, a critical mass of voters and politicians could make political integrity their first priority. Just imagine a new phase of the civil rights movement that would abolish class government and punish corruption. That's the energy from which a separation of business and state would arise.

In this scenario, Trump goes down in history as having underestimated the people and misjudged our political tradition. He becomes the spark that finally reignites political consciousness, a conflagration that plutocracy and kleptocracy could never survive.

Awakenings of this magnitude can be scary and unsettling, like other forms of rebirth. That's why Virgil is so important. Reaching the gate of Hell, he instructs Dante, "Here all your doubt is to be left behind, here all your cowardice is to fall dead."[119] Dante relies on these words as he begins the descent into the eighth circle. So steep is the slope that Virgil summons a creature called the Geryon to transport them down to the bottom:

> "Behold the beast with the pointed tail, who can pass over mountains, who breaks walls and weaponry, who makes the world a festering morass!" . . . Fraud's filthy image came to us . . . His face was the face of a just man, so benign was the outward aspect that it chose to wear, but beneath it his long trunk was serpentine . . . His breast and back and both sides were arrayed with painted knots and ringlets . . . that worst of all beasts . . . The entire length of his tail was quivering in the emptiness and lifting its forked end, which had its point armed like a scorpion's sting.[120]

Couldn't these be the features hidden beneath Trump's capacious business suits? The serpentine trunk, hairy paws, and forked tail are very much like Trump's racism, sexism, and authoritarianism—repulsive features that serve the Beast's corrupt purposes. Everyone could be right that Trump is multifaceted without contradicting the thesis that, fundamentally, he's the spirit of infinite greed.

When the time comes to mount the Geryon, Virgil urges Dante, "Be bold, and let your soul be fortified."[121] Flying on its back "with nothing but the beast in view," Dante admits "Such fear, I think, did no one ever feel."[122] And yet he keeps his eyes open and his mind clear, learning what he must.

Choosing revolution means making Trump our Geryon instead of our president. He's provided us with an up close and personal tour of the eighth circle of Hell; and so long as we continue to rationalize or deny what we've seen, he'll confine us here. Though most of us didn't choose this fate in 2016, it came through the corruption that we and our nation allowed. But by changing our laws, institutions, and political culture to account for such greed and abuse, we can climb—over Trump, over the political systems of plutocracy and kleptocracy—into a world of light.

The time has come to open our eyes, acknowledge our vulnerability, and make corruption our teacher. It's in our power to choose this dark night, allow our cowardice to fall dead, and let the national soul be fortified.

NOTES

PREFACE

1. United States Department of Justice, "Declassification: Frequently Asked Questions," September 13, 2016, https://www.justice.gov/open/declassification/declassification-faq.

CHAPTER 1

1. Subhamoy Das, "The Parable of Six Blind Men and the Elephant," *Learn Religions*, accessed August 15, 2018, https://www.learnreligions.com/six-blind-men-and-the-elephant-1770380.

2. Lindsey Bever, "Franklin Graham: The Media Didn't Understand the 'God-Factor' in Trump's Win," *Washington Post*, November 10, 2016.

3. Ryan Lovelace, "Billionaire GOP Donor Compares Trump to King David," *Washington Examiner*, June 30, 2016.

4. Jane Coaston, "The 'Biblical' Defense of Trump's Affair with Stormy Daniels," *Vox.com*, March 26, 2018.

5. Donald J. Trump (@realDonaldTrump), accessed August 21, 2019, https://twitter.com/realDonaldTrump/status/1164138795475881986.

6. Robert E. Lerner, "Antichrist," *Encyclopedia Britannica*, accessed December 10, 2019.

7. Samuel Thorpe, "Farrakhan Compares Trump to Satan during Visit to Iran," *Jerusalem Post*, November 5, 2018; Joe Concha, "Maher Compares Trump to 'Father of Lies' Satan," *The Hill*, August 5, 2017; John Agar, "Angry Man with 'Trump Is Satan' Sign: Police Search Home for Explosives," *MLive*, November 2, 2018.

8. "Trump Calls Clinton 'the Devil,'" *BBC*, August 2, 2016.

9. John T. Jost et al., "System Justification: How Do We Know It's Motivated?" in *The Psychology of Justice and Legitimacy: The Ontario Symposium Volume 11*, eds. D. Ramona Bobocel et al. (New York, Psychology Press, 2010), 191.

10. Danielle Gaucher, Aaron C. Kay, and Kristin Laurin, "The Power of the Status Quo," in Bobocel et al., *The Psychology of Justice and Legitimacy*, 155.

11. Ibid.

12. Jost et al., "System Justification," 191.

13. Saxe and Ramakrishna, in Das, "Six Blind Men and the Elephant."

14. Rev. 13, New International Version.

CHAPTER 2

1. Rev. 12:7–10, New International Version (NIV).

2. "Classification of Demons," Wikipedia, accessed March 1, 2019.

3. Matt. 6:19–21, 24 (KJV).

4. See: "The Gospel of Matthew: General Introduction," Yale University, https://divinity.yale.edu/sites/default/files/sections-introduction.pdf.

5. Matt. 6:23 (KJV).

6. Britt Peterson, "Why Donald Trump Trumps Donald Drumpf," *Boston Globe*, September 9, 2015.

7. Jerry Useem, "What Does Donald Trump Really Want?," *Fortune*, April 3, 2000.

8. Peterson, "Why Donald Trump Trumps Donald Drumpf."

9. Joel Gunter, "Right to Bear Arms? Trump Accused of Plagiarizing Family Crest," *BBC*, May 31, 2017.

10. David Barstow, Susanne Craig, and Russ Buettner, "Trump Engaged in Suspect Tax Schemes as He Reaped Riches from His Father," *New York Times*, October 2, 2018.

11. Josh Hafner, "Judge Finalizes $25 Million Trump University Settlement for Students of 'Sham University,'" *USA Today*, April 10, 2018.

12. Kate Taylor, "Porn Star Stormy Daniels Is Taking a Victory Lap after Michael Cohen's Guilty Plea. Here's a Timeline of Trump's Many Marriages and Rumoured Affairs," *Business Insider Australia*, August 23, 2018.

13. French-English translation at: "English Translation of 'Tromper,'" *Collins Dictionary*, accessed March 1, 2019.

14. Michael Balsamo, "Trump Directed Illegal Payments to Buy Silence of Two Women during Campaign, Prosecutors Say," *Chicago Tribune*, December 8, 2018.

15. Susanne Craig (@susannecraig), "'I got peanuts' from my dad, Donald Trump has said. Our investigation found Trump received the equivalent today of at least $413 million from his dad and at least another $61 million in loans. Not $1 million—at least $61 million," October 2, 2018.

16. "Trump," *Merriam-Webster*, accessed March 1, 2019.

17. Ibid.

18. "Donald J. Trump," *Amazon.com*, accessed March 1, 2019.

19. Amazon, "Donald J. Trump."

20. Christina Cheddar Berk, "Donald Trump . . . the Fragrance," *CNBC*, March 19, 2012.

21. Tessa Stuart, "A Timeline of Donald Trump's Creepiness while He Owned Miss Universe," *Rolling Stone*, October 12, 2016.

22. Daniel Victor, "'Access Hollywood' Reminds Trump: 'The Tape Is Very Real,'" *New York Times*, November 28, 2017.

23. Useem, "What Does Donald Trump Really Want?"

24. G. W. Lorein, *The Antichrist Theme in the Intertestamental Period* (London: T & T Clark International, 2003), 27.

25. "Mammonist," *Merriam-Webster*, accessed December 10, 2019.

26. Danny Hakim, "The Coat of Arms Said 'Integrity.' Now It Says 'Trump,'" *New York Times*, May 28, 2017.

27. David Edward Tabachnick and Toivo Koivukoski, "Preface: Understanding Oligarchy," in *On Oligarchy: Ancient Lessons for Global Politics*, eds. David Tabachnick and Toivo Koivukoski (Toronto: University of Toronto Press, 2011), ix.

28. Dan Kopf, "The Typical US Congress Member Is 12 Times Richer than the Typical American Household," *Quartz*, February 13, 2018.

29. Ethan Wolff-Mann, "Donald Trump Has More Money than Every US President Combined," *Money*, September 25, 2015.

30. Melissa Yeager, "The Trump Question: How Do Self-Financing Candidates Fare in Elections?," *Sunlight Foundation*, August 28, 2015.

31. Alan Feuer, "Trump Ordered to Pay $2 Million to Charities for Misuse of Foundation," *New York Times*, November 7, 2019.

32. On 2016: Kenneth P. Vogel and Isaac Arnsdorf, "Trump's Campaign Paid His Businesses $8.2 Million," *Politico*, September 22, 2016; on the midterms: Russ Choma, "Trump Campaign Paid Millions to Trump Businesses during Midterms," *Mother Jones*, November 14, 2018; on 2020: Dan Alexander,

"How Donald Trump Shifted $1.1M of Campaign-Donor Money into His Business," *Forbes*, December 6, 2018.

33. Useem, "What Does Donald Trump Really Want?"

34. Ezra Klein, "Trump: 'My whole life I've been greedy . . . Now I want to be greedy for the United States,'" *Vox*, January, 29 2016.

35. Richard C. Paddock et al., "Potential Conflicts of Interest around the Globe for Trump, the Businessman President," *New York Times*, November 26, 2016.

36. Glenn Kessler and Michelle Ye Hee Lee, "Trump's Claim That the President 'Can't Have a Conflict of Interest,'" *Washington Post*, November 23, 2016.

37. The Editorial Board, "What Is Donald Trump Hiding?," *New York Times*, May 8, 2019.

38. BBC News, "Donald Trump: A List of Potential Conflicts of Interest," *BBC*, April 18, 2017.

39. Kurt Eichenwald, "How the Trump Organization's Foreign Business Ties Could Upend U.S. National Security," *Newsweek*, September 14, 2016.

40. Emily Shugerman, "Trump's Federal Ethics Chief Resigns after Clashing with President," *Independent*, July 6, 2017.

41. Eric Lipton, "New Ethics Chief Has Fought to Roll Back Restrictions," *New York Times*, July 26, 2017.

42. Rachael Revesz, "Donald Trump's Conflicts of Interest Are Making the US Government Seem a 'Kleptocracy', Says Former White House Ethics Chief," *Independent*, July 31, 2017.

43. The Constitutional Accountability Center, "Blumenthal, et al. v. Trump," https://www.theusconstitution.org/litigation/trump-and-foreign-emoluments-clause/.

44. U.S. Const. art. I, § 9.

45. Congressional Research Service, "The Emoluments Clauses of the U.S. Constitution," October 16, 2019.

46. U.S. Const. art. II, § 1, cl. 7.

47. Sharon LaFraniere, "U.S. Appeals Court Reinstates Emoluments Case against Trump," *New York Times*, September 13, 2019.

48. Rebecca Ballhaus, "Trump's Wealthy Appointments Contrast with Populist Campaign Tone," *Wall Street Journal*, December 1, 2016.

49. Kenneth P. Vogel and Madeline Conway, "Trump on Cabinet: 'I want people that made a fortune,'" *Politico*, December 8, 2016.

50. See Shawn Donnan, "Trump's Wealthy Cabinet Choices Hark Back to Gilded Age," *Financial Times*, December 2, 2016.

51. Manu Raju, "First on CNN: Trump's Cabinet Pick Invested in Company, Then Introduced a Bill to Help It," *CNN*, January 17, 2017.

CHAPTER 3

1. Frank Newport, "2017 Update on Americans and Religion," *Gallup*, December 22, 2017.

2. Gen. 3:16–19, New International Version (NIV).

3. Gen. 3:21–22, (NIV).

4. 60,000 years estimate: "Map of Human Migration," *National Geographic*, accessed October 5, 2019; prior estimate: Ewen Callaway, "Oldest *Homo sapiens* Fossil Claim Rewrites Our Species' History," *Nature*, June 7, 2017.

5. Callaway, "Oldest *Homo sapiens* Fossil Claim."

6. Heidi Ledford, "Back When the Desert Was Green," *Nature*, August 14, 2008.

7. Pallab Ghosh, "Modern Humans Left Africa Much Earlier," *BBC*, January 25, 2018.

8. April Nowell, "Cognition, Behavioral Modernity, and the Archaeological Record of the Middle and Early Upper Paleolithic," in *Evolution of Mind, Brain, and Culture*, eds.

Gary Hatfield and Holly Pittman (Philadelphia: University of Pennsylvania Press, 2013), 236.

9. Erin Wayman, "When Did the Human Mind Evolve to What It Is Today?," *Smithsonian.com*, June 25, 2012.

10. UF News, "UF Study of Lice DNA Shows Humans First Wore Clothes 170,000 Years Ago," January 6, 2011.

11. Ian Gilligan, *Climate, Clothing, and Agriculture in Prehistory: Linking Evidence, Causes, and Effects* (Cambridge: Cambridge University Press 2018), 123.

12. Simon Neubauer, Jean-Jacques Hublin, and Philipp Gunz, "Modern Human Brain Organization Emerged Only Recently," Max-Planck-Gesellschaft, January 24, 2018.

13. Ronald Hendel, *The Book of Genesis: A Biography* (Princeton, NJ: Princeton University Press 2019), 32–33.

14. Luke 4:5–6, King James Version (KJV).

15. 1 Pet. 5:8 (KJV).

16. Eph. 6:12 (KJV).

17. Matt. 6:24 (KJV).

18. Luke 16:13 (KJV). As with Matt. 6:24, some translations use the word *money*, while others use the word *Mammon*.

19. John 2:13–16, New Revised Standard Version (NRSV).

20. Ken Baker, *The Company of Jesus* (Lulu.com, 2017), 350.

21. Matt. 26:15–16 (NIV).

22. Luke 23:2 (NIV).

23. Reza Aslan, *Zealot: The Life and Times of Jesus of Nazareth* (Allen & Unwin, 2013), 34–35.

24. Luke 23:14–21 (NIV).

25. Aslan, *Zealot*, 34–35; 60,000 soldiers and "cruelty and corruption" in: Graham Land, "66 AD: Was the Great Jewish Revolt against Rome a Preventable Tragedy?," *History Hit*, July 30, 2018.

26. Ramsay MacMullen, *Corruption and the Decline of Rome* (New Haven, CT: Yale University Press, 1988), v.

27. Edward Gibbon, *The History of the Decline and Fall of the Roman Empire*, vol. 6, 60 (1788).

28. MacMullen, *Corruption and the Decline of Rome*, 122–70.

29. *The Constitutional Documents of the Puritan Revolution, 1625–1660, ed.* Samuel Rawson Gardiner (Oxford: Oxford University Press, 1906), 373–74.

30. C. N. Trueman, "The Trial and Execution of Charles I," *History Learning Site*, March 17, 2015.

31. Stephen C. Manganiello, *The Concise Encyclopedia of the Revolutions and Wars of England, Scotland, and Ireland, 1639–1660* (Lanham, MD: Scarecrow Press, 2004), 543.

32. Ibid.

33. "Eikonoklastes," The John Milton Reading Room, Dartmouth College, accessed April 25, 2019.

34. Milton, *Paradise Lost*, bk. 1, lines 36–41, 43.

35. Ibid., line 58.

36. Ibid., bk. 4, lines 806–7.

37. Ibid., bk. 1, line 47. Compare to Rev. 12:7–10 (NIV).

38. Ibid. lines 61–62, 67, 72–74.

39. Ibid., line 796.

40. Ibid., bk. 2, lines 368–70.

41. Ibid., lines 380–84.

42. Ibid., bk. 4, 89–90.

43. Ibid., line 531.

44. Laura Lunger Knoppers, "Late Political Prose," in *A Companion to Milton*, ed. Thomas N. Corns (Malden, MA: Blackwell Publishing, 2003), 316.

45. Ibid.

46. Ibid., 317.

47. "Eikonoklastes," The John Milton Reading Room, Dartmouth College, accessed April 25, 2019.

48. Knoppers, "Late Political Prose," 324.

49. John Milton, "The Ready and Easy Way to Establish a Free Commonwealth," in *The Prose Works of John Milton, Volume 2*, ed. Evert Modercai Clark (New Haven, CT: Yale University Press, 1847, originally published in 1660), 179.

50. Milton, *Paradise Lost*, bk. 12, lines 562–71.

51. Ibid., lines 583–84.

52. Ibid., lines 586–87.

53. John Locke, *Two Treatises of Government*, ed. Peter Laslett (Cambridge: Cambridge University Press, 1988), 400.

54. Dred Scott v. Sandford, 60 U.S. 393, 407 (1857).

55. Coppage v. Kansas, 236 U.S. 1, 17 (1915).

56. "Henry Wilson," Encyclopedia Britannica.

57. Henry Ward Beecher, *Freedom and War: Discourses on Topics Suggested by the Times* (Boston: Ticknor and Fields, 1863), 380–81.

58. M. W. Howard, *The American Plutocracy* (New York: Holland Publishing Co., 1895), 3.

59. Howard, *The American Plutocracy*, 103.

60. R. F. Pettigrew, *Triumphant Plutocracy* (New York: The Academy Press, 1922), 370–71.

61. Joseph Fishkin and William E. Forbath, "Wealth Commonwealth and The Constitution of Opportunity," in *Wealth: NOMOS LVIII*, eds. Jack Knight and Melissa Schwartzberg (New York: NYU Press, 2017), 73.

62. Franklin D. Roosevelt, "Acceptance Speech for the Renomination for the Presidency" (June 27, 1936), *The American Presidency Project*.

63. Locke, *Two Treatises of Government*, 400.

64. John Rawls, *A Theory of Justice* (Cambridge, MA: Belknap Press, 1971).

65. Buckley v. Valeo, 424 U.S. 1 (1976).

66. Ibid.

67. John Goodwin, *Theomachia; Or the Grand Imprudence of Men Running the Hazard of Fighting against God, in Suppressing Any Way, Doctrine, or Practice, Concerning Which They Know Not Certainly Whether It Be from God Or No* (1644).

68. *Divine Right and Democracy*, ed. David Wotton (Indianapolis: Hackett Publishing Co., 2003), 265.

69. *A Complete Collection of the Historical, Political and Miscellaneous Works of John Milton* (Printed for A. Miller at Buchanan's Head, 1738), 159.

70. Milton, *Paradise Lost*, bk. 1, lines 679–84.

71. Ibid., bk. 2, lines 252–60.

72. Ibid., lines 274–77, 280–81.

CHAPTER 4

1. On cooperation: Yuval N. Harari, *Sapiens: A Brief History of Mankind* (London: Vintage Books, 2015); on virgins: Ronald Tiersky, "ISIS's Deadliest Weapon Is the Idea of Heaven," *Huffpost*, September 22, 2017.

2. Center for Responsive Politics, "Did Money Win?" *OpenSecrets.Org*, accessed October 1, 2019.

3. Nicholas Confessore, Sarah Cohen, and Karen Yourish, "The Families Funding the 2016 Presidential Election," *New York Times*, October 10, 2015.

4. Center for Responsive Politics, "Donor Demographics—2018," *OpenSecrets.Org*, accessed December 10, 2019.

5. Center for Responsive Politics, "Donor Demographics—1990," *OpenSecrets.Org*.

6. David Roberts, "Political Donors in the US are Whiter, Wealthier, and More Conservative than Voters," *Vox*, December 9, 2016.

7. Clyde Wilcox, "Contributing as Political Participation," in *A Users Guide to Campaign Finance Reform*, ed. Gerald C.

Lubenow (Lanham, MD: Rowman & Littlefield, 2001), 115–19; Benjamin I. Page and Martin Gilens, *Democracy in America? What Has Gone Wrong and What We Can Do about It* (Chicago: The University of Chicago Press, 2017).

8. Sean McElwee, "Whose Voice, Whose Choice? The Distorting Influence of the Political Donors Class in Our Big-Money Elections," *Demos*, December 8, 2016.

9. Robert Pear, "In House, Many Spoke with One Voice: Lobbyists,'" *New York Times*, November 15, 2009.

10. Mike McIntire, "Conservative Nonprofit Acts as a Stealth Business Lobbyist," *New York Times*, April 21, 2012.

11. Davis v. Federal Election Commission, 554 U.S. 724 (2008) at 742.

12. Citizens United v. Federal Election Commission, 558 U.S. 310 (2010) at 354–360.

13. Meredith McGehee, "Only a Tiny Fraction of Americans Give Significantly to Campaigns," *Campaign Legal Center*, October 18, 2012.

14. Carrie Levine, "Surprise! No. 1 Super PAC Backs Democrats," *Center for Public Integrity*, November 3, 2014.

15. Kay Lehman Schlozman, Sidney Verba, and Henry E. Brady, *The Unheavenly Chorus: Unequal Political Voice and the Broken Promise of American Democracy* (Princeton, NJ: Princeton University Press, 2012), 593.

16. Lee Drutman, "How Corporate Lobbyists Conquered American Democracy," *Atlantic*, April 20, 2015.

17. Lee Drutman, *The Business of America Is Lobbying: How Corporations Became Politicized and Politics Became More Corporate* (New York: Oxford University Press, 2015), 13.

18. Bill Allison and Sarah Harkins, "Fixed Fortunes: Biggest Corporate Political Interests Spend Billions, Get Trillions," *Sunlight Foundation*, November 17, 2014.

19. Wilcox, "Contributing as Political Participation," 115–19.

20. McCutcheon v. FEC, 572 U.S. 185 (2014).

21. McCutcheon, 572 U.S. at 1441 (quoting Citizens United v. Federal Election Commission, 558 U.S. 310 (2010) at 360).

22. Sahil Kapur, "Scholar Behind Viral 'Oligarchy' Study Tells You What It Means," *Talking Points Memo*, April 22, 2014.

23. Martin Gilens and Benjamin I. Page, "Testing Theories of American Politics: Elites, Interest Groups, and Averages Citizens," *Perspectives on Politics* 12, no. 3 (September 2014), 564.

24. Gilens and Page, "Testing Theories of American Politics," 567.

25. Thomas Piketty, *Capital in the Twenty-First Century*, trans. Arthur Goldhammer (Cambridge, MA: Harvard University Press, 2014), 257.

26. Timothy K. Kuhner, "The Third Coming of American Plutocracy: Reforming Campaign Finance in America," in *Democracy by the People*, eds. Eugene D. Mazo and Timothy K. Kuhner (Cambridge: Cambridge University Press, 2018).

27. Piketty, *Capital in the Twenty-First Century*, 24, 173.

28. Jojanneke van der Toorn et al., "A Sense of Powerlessness Fosters System Justification: Implications for the Legitimation of Authority, Hierarchy, and Government," *Political Psychology* 36, no. 1 (February, 2015) (first published online April 22, 2014).

29. Tina Nguyen, "You Could Fit All the Voters Who Cost Clinton the Election into a Mid-Size Football Stadium," *Vanity Fair*, December 1, 2016.

30. Lindsey Cook, "Here's Who Paid Hillary Clinton $22 Million in Speaking Fees," *U.S. News*, April 22, 2016.

31. "Money Raised as of December 31," *Washington Post*, accessed December 15, 2017; Matt Rhoades, "How the Clinton Foundation Brought Down Hillary's Campaign," *New York Post*, November 17, 2016.

32. Nicholas Confessore and Rachel Shorey, "Democrats Rake in Money, Thanks to Suit by Republicans," *New York Times*, September 30, 2016.

33. *Washington Post*, "Money Raised as of December 31."

34. Ibid.

35. Buckley v. Valeo, 424 U.S. 1 (1976) at 51–54.

36. David A. Graham, "The Lie of Trump's 'Self-Funding' Campaign," *Atlantic*, May 13, 2016.

37. *Washington Post*, "Money Raised as of December 31."

38. Eric Lichtblau, "'Super PACs' Spent Millions before Candidates Announced, Filings Show," *New York Times*, July 31, 2015.

39. The Editorial Board, "Republicans Audition for Big Money," *New York Times*, July 31, 2015.

40. Wendy R. Weiser, "Voter Suppression: How Bad? (Pretty Bad)," *American Prospect*, October 1, 2014.

41. Shelby County v. Holder, 570 U.S. 529 (2013).

42. Shelby County, p18 (slip opinion).

43. Weiser, "Voter Suppression."

44. Ibid.

45. Tomas Lopez, "'Shelby County': One Year Later," *Brennan Center for Justice*, June 24, 2014.

46. Niraj Chokshi, "Map: 22 States Have Passed New Voting Restrictions over the Past Four Years," *Washington Post*, June 17, 2014.

47. Wendy R. Weiser and Erik Opsal, "The State of Voting in 2014," *Brennan Center for Justice*, June 17, 2014.

48. Michael Keller and Yvette Romero, "The Definitely Messy, Probably Solvable Reasons Americans Don't Vote," *Bloomberg*, April 4, 2016.

49. Michelle Alexander, *The New Jim Crow: Mass Incarceration in the Age of Colorblindness* (New York: The New Press, 2010).

50. Ben Kamisar, "Trump Tweets Stir Debate on Intimidation," *The Hill*, December 10, 2016.

51. Jonah Goldberg, "Just Because Trump Is 'Anti-PC' Doesn't Mean We Should Celebrate His Vulgarity," *National Review*, January 30, 2016.

52. Terry Collins, "'Alt-right's Spencer Is Back on Twitter. Is Hate Speech, Too?" *CNET*, December 13, 2016; T. A. Frank, "How the Alt-Right Became the Party of Hate," *Vanity Fair*, August 31, 2016.

53. Eric Lipton, David E. Sanger, and Scott Shane, "The Perfect Weapon: How Russian Cyberpower Invaded the U.S," *New York Times*, December 13, 2016.

54. Stanley Feldman and Melissa Herrmann, "CBS News Exit Polls: How Donald Trump Won the U.S. Presidency," *CBS News*, November 9, 2016.

55. Andrew Higgins, Mike McIntire, and Gabriel J. X. Dance, "Inside a Fake News Sausage Factory: 'This Is All about Income,'" *New York Times*, November 25, 2016.

56. Guardian Staff and Agencies, "Washington Gunman Motivated by Fake News 'Pizzagate' Conspiracy," *Guardian*, December 5, 2016.

57. Tom Jensen, "Trump Remains Unpopular; Voters Prefer Obama on SCOTUS Pick," *Public Policy Polling*, December 9, 2016.

58. Landon Thomas Jr., "Financier Starts Sentence in Prostitution Case," *New York Times*, July 1, 2008.

59. Landon Thomas Jr., "Jeffrey Epstein: International Moneyman of Mystery," *New York Magazine*, October 28, 2002.

60. Annie Karni, Eileen Sullivan, and Noam Scheiber, "Acosta to Resign as Labor Secretary over Jeffrey Epstein Plea Deal," *New York Times*, July 12, 2019.

61. Maggie Haberman and Annie Karni, "Trump and Epstein Partied and Commented on Women in 1992 Video," *New York Times*, July 17, 2019.

62. Alan Yuhas, "Woman Who Accuses Donald Trump of Raping Her at 13 Drops Lawsuit," *Guardian*, November 5, 2016.

63. Rory Carroll, "Woman Accusing Trump of Raping Her at 13 Cancels Her Plan to Go Public," *Guardian*, November 3, 2016.

64. John Bowden, "Trump Jr. Questions Circumstances around Jeffrey Epstein's Death," *The Hill*, October 31, 2019.

65. Michael Gold, Danielle Ivory, and Nicole Hong, "Guards Accused of Napping and Shopping Online the Night Epstein Died," *New York Times*, November 19, 2019.

66. Seung Min Kim and Hannah Knowles, "Trump Retweets Conspiracy Theory Tying the Clintons to Epstein's Death," *Washington Post*, August 11, 2019.

67. "Corruption," *Lexico*, accessed November 1, 2019; "Corruption," *Merriam-Webster*, accessed November 1, 2019.

68. Glenn Kessler, Salvador Rizzo, and Meg Kelly, "President Trump made 16,241 false or misleading claims in his first three years," *Washington Post*, January 20, 2020.

69. Harry G. Frankfurt, *On Bullshit* (Princeton, NJ: Princeton University Press, 2005), 56.

70. Ibid., 37.

71. Ibid., 22–23.

72. Ibid., 64–65.

73. Adam Lusher, "Cambridge Analytica: Who Are They, and Did They Really Help Trump Win the White House?" *Independent*, March 21, 2018.

74. Nicole Puglise, "Exit Polls and Election Results—What We Learned," *Guardian*, November 12, 2016.

75. Feldman and Herrmann, "CBS News Exit Polls."

76. Ibid.

77. "2016 Election Exit Polls," *Washington Post*, November 29, 2016.

78. Mark R. Reiff, "The Difference Principle, Rising Inequality, and Supply-Side Economics: How Rawls Got Hijacked by the Right," *Revue de Philosophie Economique* 13, no. 2 (2012): 124.

79. John T. Jost, Mahzarin R. Banaji, and Brian A. Nosek, "A Decade of System Justification Theory: Accumulated Evidence of Conscious and Unconscious Bolstering of the Status Quo," *Political Psychology* 25, no. 6 (November 2004): 887.

80. Feldman and Herrmann, "CBS News Exit Polls."

81. Ronald Inglehart and Pippa Norris, "Trump, Brexit, and the Rise of Populism: Economics Have-Nots and Cultural Backlash." IDEAS Working Paper Series from RePEc. Harvard University, Cambridge, MA, August 2016.

82. John T. Jost et al., "System Justification: How Do We Know It's Motivated?" in *The Psychology of Justice and Legitimacy: The Ontario Symposium Volume 11*, eds. D. Ramona Bobocel et al. (New York: Psychology Press, 2010), 176.

83. Alex Beam, "I Dream of Donald Trump," *Boston Globe*, May 15, 2017.

84. Jost, Banaji, and Nosek, "A Decade of System Justification Theory," 883.

85. Jost et al., "System Justification: How Do We Know It's Motivated," 174.

86. van der Toorn et al., "A Sense of Powerlessness Fosters System Justification."

87. Ibid., 3.

88. Ibid., 15.

89. Gaurav Khanna, "Rotating Black Holes May Serve as Gentle Portals for Hyperspace Travel," *Phys.org*, January 9, 2019.

CHAPTER 5

1. John Burnett, "Almost 15,000 Migrant Children Now Held at Nearly Full Shelters," *NPR*, December 13, 2018.

2. Alan Gomez, "Democrats Grill Trump Administration Officials over Family Separation Policy on the Border," *USA Today*, February 7, 2019.

3. Priscilla Alvarez, "House Report: At Least 18 Migrant Children under the Age of 2 Were Separated from Parents for 20 Days to 6 Months," *CNN*, July 12, 2019; H.R. Rep. No. (2019).

4. Caitlin Dickerson, "'There Is a Stench': Soiled Clothes and No Baths for Migrant Children at a Texas Center," *New York Times*, June 21, 2019.

5. Caitlin Owens, Stef W. Knight, and Harry Stevens, "Thousands of Migrant Youth Allegedly Suffered Sexual Abuse in U.S. Custody," *Axios*, February 27, 2019.

6. Meagan Flynn, "Detained Migrant Children Got No Toothbrush, No Soap, No Sleep. It's No Problem, Government Argues," *Washington Post*, June 21, 2019; Camilo Montoya-Galvez, "Here's Why the Trump Administration Says It's Not Required to Give Migrant Children Soap," *CBS News*, June 24, 2019.

7. Miriam Jordan, "Inspectors Find Nooses in Cells at Immigration Detention Facility," *New York Times*, October 2, 2018.

8. Guardian staff and agencies, "Texas Migrant Detention Facilities 'Dangerously Overcrowded'—US Government Report," *Guardian;* Adam Serwer, "A Crime By Any Name," *Atlantic*, July 3, 2019.

9. Severin Carrell, "US Taxpayers Shelling Out Millions for Luxury Hotels for Trump State Visit," *Guardian*, June 4, 2019; "Luxurious London Hotel With Royal Connections in Exclusive Mayfair," Intercontinental Hotels & Resorts, accessed November 8, 2019.

10. Emily J. Fox, "Donald Trump's Lifestyle Could Cost Taxpayers Nearly $1 Billion," *Vanity Fair*, April 11, 2017.

11. Michal Kranz, "Melania Trump's Security Detail at Trump Tower Cost Taxpayers More Than $100,000 a Day," *Business Insider Australia*, January 30, 2018.

12. Eric Schaal, "Here Are the Ways Trump Cashes in on Being President," *Showbiz CheatSheet*, January 14, 2019.

13. Brad Heath, "Trump Picks Golf Club, Mar-a-Lago Members as Ambassadors," *USA Today*, February 8, 2019.

14. Julia Ainsley, "Trump Admin's 'Tent Cities' Cost More Than Keeping Migrant Kids with Parents," *NBC News*, June 20, 2018.

15. Luke Darby, "Trump's Child Detention Camps Cost $775 Per Person Every Day," *GQ*, January 25, 2019.

16. Yeganeh Torbati and Kristina Cooke, "First Stop for Migrant Kids: For-Profit Detention Center," *Reuters*, February 15, 2019.

17. Alex Wayne, Jennifer Epstein, and Jonathan Levin, "Trump's Immigrant Child Detentions Mean $458 Million for Nonprofit," *Bloomberg*, June 20, 2018.

18. Brendan Fischer and Maggie Christ, "Americans Left in the Dark over Reasons behind Private Prison Policy Reversal," *Campaign Legal Center*, December 8, 2017; Geoff West, "Politicians Shun GEO Group Contributions," *OpenSecrets.org*, July 20, 2018.

19. Manuel Madrid, "New Senate Bill Could Eliminate Tax Breaks for Private-Prison Giant GEO Group," *Miami New Times*, June 19, 2019.

20. Campaign Legal Center, "Americans Left in the Dark over Reasons behind Private Prison Policy Reversal."

21. Ibid.

22. Madrid, "New Senate Bill Could Eliminate Tax Breaks for Private-Prison Giant GEO Group."

23. Campaign Legal Center, "Americans Left in the Dark Over Reasons Behind Private Prison Policy Reversal."

24. Amy Brittain and Drew Harwell, "Private-Prison Giant, Resurgent in Trump Era, Gathers at President's Resort," *Washington Post*, October 25, 2017.

25. David Smith, "Trump Will Personally Save up to $15m under Tax Bill, Analysis Finds," *Guardian*, December 21, 2017.

26. Nicholas Confessore, Nicholas Fandos, and Rachel Shorey, "Trump Inaugural Drew Big Dollars from Donors with Vested Interests," *New York Times*, April 19, 2017.

27. Confessore, Fandos and Shorey, "Trump Inaugural Drew Big Dollars from Donors with Vested Interests."

28. Oliver Milman and Dominic Rushe, "New EPA Head Scott Pruitt's Emails Reveal Close Ties with Fossil Fuel Interests," *Guardian*, February 22, 2017.

29. New York Times Editorial Board, "Money Talked the Loudest at Donald Trump's Inauguration," *New York Times*, April 24, 2017.

30. Glenn Thrush and Coral Davenport, "Donald Trump Budget Slashes Funds for E.P.A. and State Department," *New York Times*, March 15, 2017.

31. Nathaniel Popper, Michael J. de la Merced, and Maggie Haberman, "Goldman Sachs to Extend Its Reach in Trump Administration," *New York Times*, December 9, 2016.

32. Eric Lipton and Binyamin Appelbaum, "Leashes Come Off Wall Street, Gun Sellers, Polluters and More," *New York Times*, March 5, 2017.

33. Erica L. Green, "DeVos Funnels Coronavirus Relief Funds to Favored Private and Religious Schools," *New York Times*, May 15, 2020.

34. Lipton and Appelbaum, "Leashes Come Off Wall Street."

35. Ibid.

36. Timothy Cama, "Trump Signs Repeal of Transparency Rule for Oil Companies," *The Hill*, February 14, 2017.

37. Karen Yourish and Larry Buchanan, "Mueller Report Shows Depth of Connections between Trump Campaign and Russians," *New York Times*, April 19, 2019.

38. Sharon LaFraniere, "Mueller Report Leaves Unanswered Questions About Contacts between Russians and Trump Aides," *New York Times*, April 18, 2019.

39. Mark Mazzetti et al., "Cohen Pleads Guilty and Detail's Trump's Involvement in Moscow Tower Project," *New York Times*, November 29, 2018.

40. Jonathan Kravis, "I Left the Justice Department after It Made a Disastrous Mistake. It Just Happened Again," *Washington Post*, May 12, 2020.

41. Mark Mazzetti, Maggie Haberman, and Michael S. Schmidt, "Moscow Skyscraper Talks Continued through 'the Day I Won,' Trump Is Said to Acknowledge," *New York Times*, January 20, 2019.

42. Ellen Nakashima, "Russian Government Hackers Penetrated DNC, Stole Opposition Research on Trump," *Washington Post*, June 14, 2016.

43. Sharon LaFraniere, Kenneth P. Vogel, and Maggie Haberman, "Manafort Accused of Sharing Trump Polling Data With Russian Associate," *New York Times*, January 8, 2019.

44. Adrian Chen, "The Agency," *New York Times Magazine*, June 2, 2015; Phillip Bump, "Timeline: How Russian Trolls Allegedly Tried to Throw the 2016 Election to Trump," *Washington Post*, February 16, 2018.

45. Lucien Bruggeman, "'I think I'd take it': In Exclusive Interview, Trump Says He Would Listen If Foreigners Offered Dirt on Opponents," *ABC News*, June 13, 2019.

46. Peter Stone, "Pressure Builds for Giuliani as Associate Enters Talks over Potential Plea Deal," *Guardian*, December 6, 2019.

47. Rebecca Ballhaus, Michael C. Bender and Vivian Salama, "Trump Ordered Ukraine Ambassador Removed after

Complaints from Giuliani, Others," *The Wall Street Journal*, October 3, 2019.

48. Jeremy Herb, Manu Raju, Sarah Murray, and Rene Marsh, "Trump Administration Officially Put Hold on Ukraine Aid Same Day as Trump Call," *CNN*, November 26, 2019.

49. Devlin Barrett, John Wagner, and Rosalind S. Helderman, "Two Business Associates of Trump's Personal Attorney Giuliani Have Been Arrested on Campaign Finance Charges," *Washington Post*, October 10, 2019.

50. Josh Dawsey, Tom Hamburger, and Ashley Parker, "Giuliani Works for Foreign Clients while Serving as Trump's Attorney," *Washington Post*, July 10, 2018.

51. Tom Hamburger and Rosalind S. Helderman, "Former Trump Campaign Chairman Paul Manafort Files as Foreign Agent for Ukraine Work," *Washington Post*, June 27, 2017.

52. Chris Megerian, David Willman, and Joseph Tanfani, "Richard Gates, Former Top Campaign Aide to Trump, Pleads Guilty in Russia Investigation," *Los Angeles Times*, February 23, 2018.

53. James Gordon Meek, "What You Need to Know about the Indictment against Michael Flynn," *ABC News*, February 20, 2019.

54. Craig Unger, "Trump's Russian Laundromat," *New Republic*, July 13, 2017.

55. Ibid.

56. "FinCEN Fines Trump Taj Mahal Casino Resort $10 Million for Significant and Long-Standing Anti-Money Laundering Violations," Financial Crimes Enforcement Network, March 6, 2015.

57. Unger, "Trump's Russian Laundromat."

58. Financial Crimes Enforcement Network, "FinCEN Fines Trump Taj Mahal Casino."

59. Emily Flitter, "Art of the Spin: Trump Bankers Question His Portrayal of Financial Comeback," *Reuters*, July 18, 2016.

60. Flitter, "Art of the Spin."

61. Ibid.

62. Ben Aris, "Remembering Russia's 1998 Financial Crisis (Op-ed)," *Moscow Times*, August 22, 2018.

63. Caleb Melby and Keri Geiger, "Behind Trump's Russia Romance, There's a Tower Full of Oligarchs," *Bloomberg*, March 16, 2017.

64. Nathan Layne et al., "Russian Elite Invested Nearly $100 Million in Trump Buildings," *Reuters*, March 17, 2017.

65. Unger, "Trump's Russian Laundromat."

66. Ibid.

67. Jonathan Chait, "Will Trump Be Meeting with His Counterpart – Or His Handler," *New York Magazine*, July 9, 2018.

68. Oren Dorell, "Donald Trump's Ties to Russia Go Back 30 Years," *USA Today*, February 15, 2017.

69. David A. Graham, "The Coincidence at the Heart of the Russia Hacking Scandal," *Atlantic*, July 13, 2018.

70. David Smith, Julian Borger, and Lauren Gambino, "Donald Trump Admits 'This Russia Thing' Part of Reasoning for Firing Comey," *Guardian*, May 12, 2017.

71. Craig Unger, *House of Trump, House of Putin: The Untold Story of Donald Trump and the Russian Mafia* (New York: Penguin, 2018).

72. Abigail Tracy, ""The President Has Been Acting On Russia's Behalf': U.S. Officials Are Shocked by Trump's Asset-Like Behavior," *Vanity Fair*, January 15, 2019.

73. Alexander Hamilton, Federalist No. 73 (1788).

74. Dante Alighieri, *Inferno*, ed. Giuseppe Mazzotta, trans. Michael Palma (New York and London: W. W. Norton & Company, 2008), 3.

75. Dante, *Inferno*, 4.

76. Attributed to John Ciardi in: Lawrence S. Cunningham, John J. Reich, and Lois Fichner-Rathus, *Culture and*

Values: A Survey of the Western Humanities, Volume 1, 8th ed. (Boston, MA: Cengage Learning, 2014), 316.

77. Dante, *Inferno*, 10.

78. Ibid., 41.

79. Ibid., 78.

80. Ibid., 77 (coating)–78 (cooked through).

81. Ibid., 130.

82. "Greed," The Free Dictionary, accessed October 1, 2019.

83. James Hamblin, "Emotions Seem to Be Detectable in Air," *Atlantic*, May 23, 2016.

84. Laura S. Underkuffler, *Captured by Evil: The Idea of Corruption in Law* (New Haven, CT: Yale University Press, 2013), 3–4.

85. Ibid., 3–4.

86. Ibid., 6.

87. Ibid., 93.

88. Andrew H. Wedeman, *Double Paradox: Rapid Growth and Rising Corruption in China* (Ithaca, NY: Cornell University Press, 2012), 61.

89. Ibid., 62.

90. David Jackson, "Ivanka Trump Gets New White House Title," *USA Today*, March 29, 2017.

91. 5 U.S. Code § 3110, Pub. L. 90–206, title II, § 221(a), Dec. 16, 1967, 81 Stat. 640; amended Pub. L. 95 454, title IX, § 906(a)(2), Oct. 13, 1978, 92 Stat. 1224. Association of American Physicians and Surgeons v. Clinton, 997 F.2d 898 (1993).

92. U.S. Department of Justice, "Application of the Anti-Nepotism Statute to a Presidential Appointment in the White House Office," Memorandum Opinion for the Counsel to the President, January 20, 2017.

93. Jon Swaine, "Company Part-Owned by Jared Kushner Got $90m from Unknown Offshore Investors since 2017," *Guardian*, June 10, 2019.

94. Jeffrey Sonnenfeld, "Trump's White House Is a Family Business. That's Not a Bad Thing," *Politico*, April 8, 2017.

95. Christal Hayes, "College Admissions Scam Rekindles Scrutiny of Kushner's Harvard Acceptance, $2.5M Pledge," *USA Today*, March 12, 2019.

96. Paul Waldman, "Trump Is Still Acting Like a Tinpot Kleptocrat. Here's a Rundown," *Washington Post*, May 29, 2018.

97. Edward Helmore, "Ivanka Trump Won China Trademarks Days before Her Father's Reversal on ZTE," *Guardian*, May 28, 2018.

98. Sarah Chayes, "Trump and the Path toward Kleptocracy," *Bloomberg*, May 23, 2017.

99. Ibid.

100. Ibid.

101. Chrystia Freeland, *Plutocrats: The Rise of the New Global Super-Rich and the Fall of Everyone Else* (New York: Penguin, 2012).

102. Ibid., 189–193, 195, 204, 207, 208, 223–227.

103. Carol D. Leonnig et al., "Trump Team Seeks to Control, Block Mueller's Russia Investigation," *Washington Post*, July 21, 2017.

104. Chayes, "Trump and the Path toward Kleptocracy."

105. U.S. Const. article. II, § 2.

106. Gregory Korte, "Trump Says He Can Pardon Himself during the Mueller Inquiry—but Maintains He's Done 'Nothing Wrong,'" *USA Today*, June 4, 2018.

107. Mary C. Lawton, "Presidential or Legislative Pardon of the President: Memorandum Opinion for the Deputy Attorney General," Department of Justice, August 5, 1974.

108. Kravis, "I Left the Justice Department After It Made a Disastrous Mistake."

109. Alan Smith, "Trump Is Quietly Moving at a Furious Pace to Secure 'The Single Most Important Legacy' of His Administration," *Business Insider*, July 27, 2017.

110. White House Briefings, "President Donald J. Trump Is Appointing a Historic Number of Federal Judges to Uphold Our Constitution as Written," November 6, 2019.

111. Chayes, "Trump and the Path toward Kleptocracy."

112. Dante, *Inferno*, 3.

113. Ibid.

114. Dante, *Inferno*, 4 (shape offered to my vision)–5 (all the rest).

115. John Locke, *Two Treatises of Government*, ed. Peter Laslett (Cambridge: Cambridge University Press, 1988), 400.

116. Thomas Jefferson to Tom Logan, November 12, 1816, in *The Writings of Thomas Jefferson*, ed. Paul L. Ford (New York: G. P. Putnam's Sons, 1892–1899), 10:69.

117. "Progressive Party Platform of 1912," *The American Presidency Project*, accessed October 1, 2019.

118. "Speech before the 1936 Democratic National Convention," *Austin Community College*, accessed October 1, 2019.

119. Dante, *Inferno*, 11.

120. Ibid., 61 (all before "Fraud's filthy image)–62 (starting with "Fraud's filthy image").

121. Ibid., 63.

122. Ibid., 64.

CPSIA information can be obtained
at www.ICGtesting.com
Printed in the USA
JSHW031349120720
6630JS00004B/17